HIDDEN HORIZONS

UNEARTHING 10,000 YEARS OF INDIAN CULTURE

HIDDEN HORIZONS

REVIEWS

"There is no doubt that the Great Indian culture has proved itself to be an immortal one since it dates back to the dawn of world history. Its unbroken continuity down the ages is a fact obvious enough to show that it surely does possess such noble and divine values which are eternal and beyond the laws of decay and death. Cruising along *Hidden Horizons*, one can rediscover and explore the glorious vistas of the bygone golden era. The visit is potent enough to project the timeless and all-embracing profile of the Indian culture beyond all doubts."

- H.H. Swami Satyamitranandji
Samanvay Seva Trust, Haridwar
Former Jagatguru Shankaracharya

"In spite of many excavations and other investigations, the history of India still remains a mystery. One reason is that still little attention has been paid to the vast ancient literature in Sanskrit, Prakrit and Pali, which contains valuable information that cannot be discarded all as mythology and legends. It can definitely be said that all researches sans deeper and critical studies of this valuable heritage would remain inadequate to reveal the facts about the oldest traditions like Vedic and Shramanic, which hold the keys not only to the highest spiritual and religious truths but also to the secular arts and sciences. The effort made in *Hidden Horizons* deserves appreciation and applause from all who are engrossed in this field. My heartiest congratulations."

- H.H. Acharya Mahaprajnaji
Jain Shwetambar Terapanth Samaj

"Hidden Horizons, through its critical voyages of discovery into ancient Indian history and spiritual wisdom, becomes a valuable guide to anyone who wants to have an understanding of what India really is and has been for ages. Its attempt to make readers acquainted not only with the antiquity but the abiding value of Vedic literature and practices is most remarkable. And since the text has both archaeological and historical evidence, its amazing findings about the Hindu view of time and of yoga, and of mathematics, astronomy and medicine are sure to shock the mind into a new awareness and a fresh understanding of the complex Indian psyche.

"Hidden Horizons will surely enable the readers to go beyond the known horizons into newer horizons. The work is an insightful and authentic re-creation of Indian civilization and thought."

- H.H. Jagadguru Sri Shivarathri Deshikendraji Mahaswamigalu
Sri Suttur Math, Mysore

"India's past is not only vast, but also incredible. Saints, scientists, poets, patriots and thinkers alike have enriched her land and contributed to global awakening. Other civilizations and cultures have sourced from the eternal Vedic resources of India.

"Hidden Horizons captures the glory and beauty of our Vedic lore. The book,

replete with precious nuggets, showcases the spiritual stamina of a land, whose past is relevant and benevolent to the present."

- H.H. Swami Tejomayanandaji
Head, Chinmaya Mission

"Swami Vivekananda urged Indians to rewrite Indian history after diving in depth into its arts, science, literature, and above all the vast world of Vedic and Sanskrit literature which contains clues to the survival of the future culture of humanity. David Frawley and N.S. Rajaram have worked in this line to rediscover India's civilization in its perfect background. They have tried to uphold that Indian civilization is the most ancient civilization of the world, that the Vedic literature is the oldest and the richest literature of a mature civilization, that the Aryan Invasion Theory was a projection of the imperialistic bias of politically powerful nations of the nineteenth century, and that the existence of the Saraswati river, now extinct due to geological upheavals, is not a myth but a historically and scientifically verified fact of today after the satellite pictures have confirmed the existence of subterranean water in the course of the ancient Saraswati river. The authors have tried to bridge a new dimension of Indian history."

- H.H. Swami Jitatmanandji
Secretary, Ramkrishna Mission

"I am so impressed by this essential book. *Hidden Horizons* is a divine task as it highlights and details the ancient, timeless and multi-faceted history of Indian culture and civilization. Whatever sphere one selects for study, one has to look to Indian heritage, for many of the most valuable insights in the history of humankind are encompassed within this ancient tradition. Additionally, more and more scientists and philosophers are discovering the convergence of ancient Indian edits and modern scientific and philosophical thinking. The time has come to make the history, wisdom, insights and teachings of this culture and country available, in an authentic, honest and comprehensive form for the benefit of humanity. May this book lead to a correct and complete understanding of the fundamental role played by India in the development of all aspects of the modern world."

- H.H. Swami Chidanand Saraswatiji
President, Parmarth Niketan, Rishikesh

"Bringing out *Hidden Horizons* is a highly laudable step. It highlights the important aspects and will give to the younger generations a most needed, correct, indepth and sound perspective about the great civilization and history of India. Familiarization with the glorious eternal Vedic culture and its spirituality will be a great boon for the youth."

- H.H. Swami Nirliptanandaji
Vice-President, Divine Life Society, Rishikesh

"Worldwide Hindu parents are concerned about the inaccuracies and negative slant found in school texts about India and Hinduism. *Hidden Horizons* not only effectively addresses common misinformation, such as the now-discredited Aryan Invasion theory, but deftly documents crucial contributions India has made in such fields as medicine, mathematics and astronomy. It is a much-needed, authoritative resource about the Hindu religion and India's ancient civilization that parents can share with children to build a pride in their heritage."

- H.H. Satguru Bodhinatha Veylanswamiji

Hinduism Today, Hawaii

"We the people of India belong to the great ancient Vedic Culture. Our Culture is to us what environment and soil are for the trees. Trees grow healthiest in the environment native to them. The deeper and stronger their roots, the greater the height of the trees. If we as a community want to be healthy and at the same time soar to great heights in all the fields of human endeavour it is necessary that we remember our Culture and be firmly rooted to it. This book *Hidden Horizons* is a great work in this direction. I wish it great success."

- H.H. Swami Nikhilananda Saraswatiji

Regional Head, Chinmaya Mission, New Delhi

"I am impressed by the depth of the study the authors seem to have carried out on a subject on which there are conflicting views, and the historical conclusions they draw from it. While, as a nation, we try to use science and technology to become a global innovation leader, we should also remember our past great cultural and spiritual heritage and be justifiably proud of it. This book admirably serves the latter purpose."

- Dr. R. Chidambaram

Principal Scientific Advisor to the Government of India

"*Hidden Horizons* is an authoritative book. It is only the publication of such a volume, prepared after being researched by globally respected authors like David Frawley (Vamdeva Shastri) and N.S. Rajaram, that can create a permanent and authentic record of history for our posterity to understand, accept and appreciate the contribution of ancient Indian history to the evolution of art, culture, literature, architecture, music, dance, medicine, astronomy, mathematics, fine arts, and more than anything else, spirituality in the entire world."

- **D.R. Kaarthikeyan**
Former Director, Central Bureau of Investigation
Former Director General, National Human Rights Commission

HIDDEN HORIZONS

UNEARTHING 10,000 YEARS OF INDIAN CULTURE

BY

Dr. David Frawley (Vamadeva Shastri)

AND

Dr. Navaratna S. Rajaram

Swaminarayan Aksharpith

Amdavad

HIDDEN HORIZONS
Unearthing 10,000 Years of Indian Culture

by Dr. David Frawley and Dr. Navaratna S. Rajaram

Inspirer: HDH Pramukh Swami Maharaj

First Edition: April 2006
First Reprint: May 2007

Copies: 7,000 (Total: 10,000)
Price: Rs. 100/-
ISBN: 81-7526-331-8

Published & Printed by
Swaminarayan Aksharpith
Shahibaug, Ahmedabad-4, India

Websites: www.swaminarayan.org
         www.akshardham.com
         www.mandir.org
         kids.baps.org

TABLE OF CONTENTS

PUBLISHER'S NOTE

Inspired and created by HDH Pramukh Swami Maharaj, Swaminarayan Akshardham fulfils the much-cherished wish of his guru, HDH Yogiji Maharaj.

Located on the banks of the sacred River Yamuna in New Delhi, Swaminarayan Akshardham is a unique monument to 10,000 years of Indian culture, history, traditions and values.

Spread throughout 100 acres, the Swaminarayan Akshardham complex is a breathtaking combination of ancient art and architecture, and modern science and technology. In addition to the majestic main monument, three well-researched and outstanding exhibition halls provide a glimpse into the vast and rich heritage of India.

This present book, *Hidden Horizons – Unearthing 10,000 years of Indian Culture,* is specifically written to complement the 'Sanskruti Vihar' exhibition, which is an enlightening 14-minute boat journey through 10,000 years of Indian history and culture.

The book provides details of now widely accepted archaeological, geological, linguistic, genetic and other evidence which proves that the Aryan Invasion Theory is totally false and that India's heritage is indigenous, dating back to at least the last Ice Age, 10,000 years ago. This account of India's true history will revive the pride of Indians everywhere for their motherland.

Today's youth are generally unaware of India's true history and the widespread damage caused by the currently taught, now disproved theories. This book will serve to correct current misunderstandings and will initiate a sea change in the social, cultural, political and spiritual outlook of all patriotic Indians.

We are deeply grateful to Dr. David Frawley (Vamadeva Shastri) and Dr. Navaratna S. Rajaram for writing this outstanding overview of India's true place in world civilization.

Finally, we feel sure that all who read this book with an open mind will certainly appreciate and accept the clear-cut evidence presented here that reclaims and confirms India's true place in world history as a nation of great antiquity.

- Swaminarayan Aksharpith

AUTHORS' PREFACE

The idea for this book dawned after a special meeting between the two authors and seven Swamis of the BAPS Swaminarayan Sanstha. At the request of Sadhu Brahmaviharidas the meeting naturally took place at the new Swaminarayan Akshardham in Delhi, as we were in Delhi for a conference. The Cultural Complex was then not quite yet finished (March 2005), and yet inspiring beyond imagination. The Swamis also honoured us with a tour of this new and spectacular monument. Nothing could have prepared us for the exhilarating experience we felt on that day.

As part of this tour, the Swamis showed us their "Ten Minute Down the Sarasvati River" display, one of their important cultural presentations on ancient India Culture, and a great production in its own right. They sought our help with the display and its information. In the ensuing dialogue the idea arose of a short book on ancient India written specifically to accompany the display. At the same time, we concluded that the book should also have a universal value as a concise, complete and well-illustrated volume that would be useful at all Hindu religious centres and, on a broader level, for the general public.

Both authors have written extensively on ancient India, in various books and articles widely published in the Indian press and in other countries, particularly the USA. The present volume allows us to summarize and update the material we have previously presented. We have also individually written on different aspects of Indian culture and Vedic sciences, not simply as specialists on history. Our perspective is of those who respect the Vedic tradition and can look at ancient India from its broader perspective.

We must emphasize that the ancient history of India still requires revision in light of both recent scientific information and a more accurate study of India's own venerable literature. Many of the commonly accepted and textbook accounts of ancient India have now been contradicted by new evidence in several fields. Whether one entirely agrees with the alternative views we have put forth or not, these old accounts can no longer be accepted without question.

To treat the revision of historical books as a kind of tampering with scriptures, as some scholars in India today are suggesting, makes no sense at all. History is man-made; it must be updated like all knowledge. All over the world, the dates for the beginning of civilization and for human populations are being pushed back in time. India cannot be exempted from such a revision. The historical accounts of fifty years ago cannot be made the last word any more than the science of fifty years ago.

On the scientific side, recent geological finds like the many urban sites along the now dry Sarasvati River, together with a greater understanding of natural history and genetics – like the dispersal of human populations from Greater India eight to ten thousand years ago – have important ramifications relative to the history and cultural development of India.

On the literary side, the recognition that the Vedas contain important spiritual, scientific and historical knowledge contradicts older European views of them as primitive and unsophisticated. Such data must be considered carefully and cannot be ignored. In this regard, we have tried to make the book engaging, examining the most difficult and disputed issues, so as to arrive at a deeper truth.

We have also aimed at a book that honours the cultural heritage of India and seeks to present that as part of the history. A great culture cannot arise from a historical vacuum or from mere borrowings from invading nomads, as many current accounts of ancient India suggest. India's culture is itself a proof of a great history.

We have tried to make the book relevant and alive for the modern reader, especially the youth. The book seeks to inspire as well as to inform, to turn the history of India into a cultural experience rather than a technical presentation only. The book is something like a 200-page ride down the Sarasvati River. Through a culture of ten thousand years, numerous sages, and the development of one of the world's greatest civilizations, it can only provide a few snapshots and summaries that address the main points.

For those who want more information on these subjects, we urge the reader to look into our other books and those given in the bibliography. (We also provide references and informative endnotes running throughout the text.) The history of India is one of the world's great cultural and spiritual adventures, which all people should study and can learn a great deal from.

We see the great Swaminarayan Akshardham in New Delhi as a living manifestation of the spirit of Sanatan Dharma...a spirit that renews and regenerates itself in age upon every age, millennium after millennium. Just as the Angkor Wat, a wonder of the world built a thousand years ago was one such manifestation, we see the Swaminarayan Akshardham today as the monument for the new millennium. This is the spirit that we have tried to capture in the book. We will be gratified if the readers can feel the grandeur and the wonder which the authors have felt in writing the book.

We thank in particular the BAPS Swaminarayan Sanstha and its humble, sagely leader HH Pramukh Swami Maharaj for allowing us this opportunity. Our hope is that our work does justice to the great civilization of India and helps renew and revitalize it for coming generations.

Dr. David Frawley (Vamadeva Shastri)
Dr. Navaratna S. Rajaram
September 2005

LIST OF ILLUSTRATIONS AND MAPS

ABBREVIATIONS

AV = Atharva Veda	RV = Rig Veda
BCE = Before Common Era	SB = Shatapath Brahmana
BP = Before Present	SYV = Shukla Yajur Veda
BU = Brihadaranyak Upanishad	TB = Taittiriya Brahmana
CE = Common Era	TS = Taittiriya Samhita
MS = Manu Smriti	YV = Yajur Veda

HIGHLIGHTS

Summary of the main points emphasized in this book

1. Natural history of tropical Asia shows that the origins of Indian civilization go back to the end of the last Ice Age, more than 10,000 years ago.

2. Archaeologically, India has the most extensive and continuous record of all ancient civilizations, much more than Egypt, Sumeria or Mesopotamia of the same time periods. Yet its role as a source of civilization has largely been ignored by the historical biases of the West.

3. The Vedic literature is the ancient world's largest, with its many thousands of pages dwarfing what little the rest of the world has been able to preserve. This literature reflects profound spiritual concepts, skill in mathematics, astronomy and medicine, special knowledge of language and grammar, and other hallmarks of a great civilization. It cannot be attributed to nomads and barbarians or to the short space of a few centuries.

4. The ancient Indian literature, the world's largest, and ancient Indian archaeology, also the ancient world's largest, must be connected. We can no longer accept the idea of Ancient India without a literature and Vedic literature reflecting no real culture or civilization. Vedic literature and its symbolizm is clearly reflected in Harappan archaeology and its artifacts.

5. Greater India, which included South India, was the home of most human populations which migrated after the end of the Ice Age when the water released by melting glaciers flooded the region around ten thousand years ago. Greater India, not the Middle East, is the likely cradle, not only of populations, but culture and agriculture as well.

6. The Sarasvati River, the dominant river in India in the post-Ice Age era, after 8000 BCE (10,000 BP), and the main site of urban ruins in ancient India, is well described in Vedic texts. It ceased to flow around 1900 BCE (3900 BP), making the Vedic culture older than this date. All stages of the development and drying up of the Sarasvati can be found in Vedic texts down to the Mahabharat, showing that the Vedic people were flourishing along the river at all phases.

7. There is no scientific or archaeological basis for any Aryan or Dravidian race, which are now discredited concepts. No skeletal remains of the so-called Aryans have ever been found in India. Whatever remains have been found are similar to the existing populations in the country going back to prehistoric times. There is no archaeological evidence of any Aryan invasion or migration into India but only the continuity of the same populations in the region and their cultural changes. This requires that we give up these old ideas and look at the data afresh apart from them.

8. Connections between Indian languages and those of Europe and Central

Asia, which can be found relative to both Sanskritic and Dravidian languages, are more likely traceable to a northwest movement out of India after the end of the Ice Age. The late ancient Aryan and Dravidian migrations, postulated to have taken place c. 1500 BCE (3500 BP), into India from Central Asia of Western linguistic theories occur too late, after populations and cultures were already formed, to result in the great changes attributed to them. Besides no records of such proposed invasions or migrations have yet been found. Archaeology, literature and science, including genetics, all contradict it.

9. Vedic spirituality of rituals, mantras, yoga and meditation, based on an understanding of the dharmic nature of all life, created the foundation for the great spiritual traditions of India. It emphasized individual experience of the Divine and spiritual practice over outer dogmas and beliefs. Such a spiritual ethos is the fruit of a great and mature ancient civilization.

10. The Hindu view of time, through the Hindu Yuga theory, connects human history with natural history of tens of thousands of years marked by periodic cataclysms and makes sense in the light of new scientific discoveries relating to natural history through genetics and climate changes. So the Hindu Yuga theory may be seen as a way of describing the renewal of habitation on earth in phase with the climate cycles.

11. This ancient, eternal Vedic culture is still relevant to the world today and

lives on in the great ashrams, mandirs and spiritual practices of India. Reclaiming this ancient spiritual heritage of India and spreading it throughout the world is one of the greatest needs of the coming planetary age, in which we must go beyond the boundaries of creed and materialistic values.

Prologue: Empire of the Spirit

HIDDEN HISTORY UNEARTHED

We are honoured to welcome the reader to a new and updated account of the ancient history of India. India is one of the oldest, greatest and most profound of all civilizations. Its contributions to human knowledge and culture is enormous and many-sided, extending to all aspects of material, intellectual and spiritual realms. India provides a wealth of wisdom, inspiration and insight that remains relevant today to all the people of the world. Yet its history is seldom studied in depth, even by Indians, and many misconceptions still exist that often prevent even a dedicated student from understanding it properly.

In what we see as a fresh and unique approach, we will introduce the reader to the essence of Indian culture along with this examination of its history. It is our view that we cannot separate the history of the region from the culture that arises through it. A journey into India's history should also be a cultural enrichment for the reader. India's culture is itself the key to its history and to the great treasures that the region has to offer the rest of the world.

Our account will trace history back to the end of the Ice Age and connect it to the development of the human species as a whole. In this regard, history is just one chapter in the story of humanity and should be rooted in that story as a whole.

Unlike most historical accounts found today, our point of view is rooted in an Indian or Bharatiya ethos. It is a history of India from an Indian perspective, from a point of view which honours India's place in the world and her vision of society. This can provide all of us with a more appropriate angle on India and its culture through which we can better appreciate it in its real perspective. We view India as a primary centre of world civilization past, present and future, not just as a footnote to events that occurred in the Western world. Our book has been written with a great respect for India's heritage, including its own approaches to history, human values and the goal of human life.

Because of its recent history of colonization, modern historians have tended to present India mainly as a beneficiary of gifts from outsiders – in other words, as a civilization that has only borrowed and built on the creative ideas originated by other cultures. But those who have studied India and its many contributions more deeply recognize the truth to be the opposite of this: India has been one of the great creative forces in the history of civilization. The noted author Philip Rawson introduces his book *The Art of Greater India* with the following words:

> The culture of India has been one of the world's most powerful civilizing forces. Countries of the Far East, including China, Korea, Japan, Tibet and Mongolia owe much of what is best in their own cultures to the inspiration of ideas imported from India. The West, too, has its own debts. But the members of that circle of civilizations beyond Burma scattered around the Gulf of Siam and the Java Sea, virtually owe their very existence to the creative influence of Indian ideas. ...No conquest or invasion, no forced conversion imposed them. They were adopted because the people saw they were good and they could use them... their code of living, their conceptions of law and kingship, their rich literature and highly evolved philosophy of life.[1]

The remarkable thing about Indian civilization, which draws its inspiration from the Vedic rishis, is that it is a living force and not just a thing of the past, dead monuments to be admired by tourists and studied by antiquarians. As John Le Mée, a French student of the Vedas observed:

> Precious stones or durable materials – gold, silver, bronze, marble, onyx or granite – have been used by most ancient people in an attempt to immortalize their achievements. Not so however the [Vedic] Aryans. They turned to what may seem the most volatile and insubstantial material of all – the spoken word – and out of this bubble of air fashioned a monument which for more than thirty, perhaps forty, centuries later stands untouched by time of the elements. [Actually, sixty to eighty centuries as we now know.] …the pyramids have been eroded by the desert wind, the marble broken by earthquakes, and the gold stolen by robbers, while the *Veda* is recited daily by an unbroken chain of generations, traveling like a great wave through the living substance of mind.[2]

THE SOUL AND SPIRIT OF HISTORY

India therefore must be approached in a spirit altogether different from the purely material perspective of politics and economics. Also we cannot separate the spiritual experience of India from its material achievements. For these reasons, this is not just another book on India. Our purpose is not simply to relate history to you in an academic or textbook manner to be read as a mere set of facts to be quickly forgotten. Our aim is to make the history of India come alive for you, to allow, as it were, Mother India – the mother of the Indian people and the mother of civilizations and much of the world's knowledge – to tell you her own story through her own creations. The book is intended not only to educate you about India, but also put you in contact with the soul of India – to discover the India within yourself as relevant to your own life and aspiration.

India's voice, like its civilization, has its particular relevance today as we look beyond the outer material boundaries that divide us to what really unites us together as a planet. This book is meant as a 'civilizational dialogue', a living journey through India's great history and what it means for all of humanity, so that we can once more connect human history to the eternal aspirations of our species.

SCIENCE AND SPIRITUALITY

India represents a civilization that has always valued knowledge, whether scientific or spiritual. It has not opposed science or religion, nor separated art and religion. It has always striven to make science spiritual and spirituality, a science. From its point of view, knowledge and practice are more important than dogma or belief.

Following this approach, we will explore the history of India as revealed both by modern science and by the traditional spiritual literature of the region. We will consider the role of natural history, geology, archaeology and genetics, on the one hand, and also show the relevance of the views of the great rishis and yogis of India and the vast literature, which they have left us, on the other. We will consider India's own historical records starting with the Vedas and Purans, and what India's own scientific heritage of astronomy, mathematics, linguistics and sociology has left us.

The book will outline how current scientific evidence about the history of India and the development of mankind is reflected in the cultural and literary traditions of India from the most ancient times. It will show how to make history relevant to both the cultural achievements of India and the spiritual aspirations of its people. This has always been the purpose of history or *itihasa* in Indian thought, which was not simply a matter of passing on dates and information, but of inspiring us towards a better life.

The model provided by great cultures of the past, like the models provided by great people from the past, can help us lead better lives today and guide us to a better future. Not only Indians but all people can learn and benefit enormously from the story of India. The story of India is anything but narrowly nationalistic. It is a key part of the global epoch of the human experience.

INDIA'S MATCHLESS HERITAGE

India represents one of the great civilizations of the world, with its own unique, diverse and profound culture going back many thousands of years. Notably, India has maintained the continuity of its culture perhaps better than any other civilization in the world, preserving its primary cultural and religious practices for over five thousand years. And this is going only by the preserved records in archaeology and written literature. By a proper reading of the Vedas and the Purans we can get a glimpse of the primordial origins going back even before the ending of the last Ice Age.

The civilization of India has always oriented itself to the spiritual life, the liberation of the spirit, as the main goal of human existence. This we see in its many great yogic, religious and philosophical traditions, and in the many yogis, sadhus, mystics and sages it has produced in every generation. Whether it is meditation, yoga *asanas*, mantras, chanting, ritual or prayer, we find all such higher subjects taken up in great detail, depth and comprehensiveness. Certainly, at a spiritual and yogic level, India can claim to be the great mother of world civilization. We find this same focus in ancient India, whether in figures in yoga postures on ancient Harappan seals or great Vedic chants to the cosmic powers.

Figure 1: Seated yogi in the mulabandhasana on a famous Harappan seal

Yet the civilization of India was rich not only spiritually but also materially. It had great wealth in agriculture, textiles, gold and gems that made it a goal for traders worldwide. It was this search for the legendary wealth of India which motivated Columbus to sail towards America in the first place and which had earlier brought Roman, Greek and Babylonian traders to the region.

According to economist Angus Maddison in *The World Economy: A Millennial Perspective* the region that today comprises the Indian Subcontinent held the largest share of the world's gross domestic product until the end of the 16th century. (India was the richest for over 75% of the world's counted calendar of history.)

Ancient India also had a powerful warrior class and its own traditions of martial arts. Complementary to the spiritual dharma was a kingly dharma to protect those leading the spiritual life and to maintain peace and prosperity for the entire region.[3] But India did not create a cult of foreign conquest. Even the king had to bow down before the ascetic and the renunciate and to retire to the forest for spiritual practices in his later years.

India today carries on this ancient spiritual and cultural heritage, which is developing anew in the modern world since India's return to its independence as a nation. India's gurus travel worldwide, with followers in every land, bringing deeper spiritual practices of yoga and meditation to all people. India's scientists are renowned worldwide for their skill and reliability. Its merchants are once more contributing to global prosperity and competing successfully in all the major cities of the world.

We will trace this great cultural current from its source at the beginning of what we know as history, and try to understand the forces and events that have shaped it and caused it to be what it is.

HISTORY ACCORDING TO AN INDIAN (BHARATIYA) SCHOOL OF THOUGHT

India has produced innumerable great thinkers and teachings, from the Vedic rishis to modern yogis, gurus and sages. It has given birth to more spiritual teachings and mystical traditions than any other region in the world, whether in terms of right action (Dharma), knowledge (*Gnan*), detachment (*Vairagya*), devotion (Bhakti), or the exploration of inner energies through the practice of yoga. These have their own points of view, and require an understanding of their own values and perceptions in order to fully comprehend them. India's traditions of history, social science, politics and human relation, are based on such spiritual views. These can be different from Western traditions that follow a more outward view of human life.

Even today, selfless spiritual leaders like Pramukh Swami Maharaj, Amritanandamayi Ma, Satya Sai Baba and many others carry forward this tradition.

Unlike some Western religious leaders who owe their eminence to the high office they hold, these spiritual figures owe their following and reverence purely for their inspiring qualities and their concern for their devotees. They rarely have counterparts in the modern West.

Our aim is to examine the history and heritage of India from an Indic or 'Bharatiya' perspective; from a perspective that reflects India's world view, which sees India as a source of civilization. This view of India as having borrowed its culture mainly from the West reflects a Western inability to understand Indian civilization. And, as is increasingly becoming clear with new evidence, it has no real scientific basis either. The Western mind has been unable to go to the depths of Indian values and understand the Indian view of the world. We hope to correct that distortion in the information presented here and to counter the confusion that it has caused.[4]

We feel that this Indic perspective – which is neglected today even inside India – is not just of value relative to history, but contains important insights relative to science, sociology, medicine and all major aspects of human behaviour. We hope to impart such an Indic or Bharatiya view of life to the reader.

SANATAN DHARMA AND THE RISHI CULTURE

India or Bharat's own school of thought and its own world view emphasizes dharma or natural law as the main factor behind both human life and the workings of the universe. It sees human history in the context of the development of life and consciousness, and not just in terms of dates, events and inventions.

The Vedic vision begins with the idea of an eternal tradition of truth, wisdom and knowledge. This, in Sanskrit, is called 'Sanatan Dharma' – the eternal dharma or way of truth. In the Vedic view, consciousness underlies the entire universe of matter, energy and mind and provides the force that motivates and moves them.

This Vedic vision has important historical ramifications. According to its view, there was a rishi or yogic culture at the beginning of human history, not only in India but throughout the world. We find the echoes of this great tradition in the many stories of the great sages, seers and prophets of ancient times – such as occur in the annals of cultures as diverse as the Mayan American, the Chinese, the Egyptian, Babylonian, Greek, Celtic and Hindu. These Hindu rishis or seers were said to have established the paths to spiritual knowledge for humanity at the beginning of this world age, which we can place roughly around the end of the last Ice Age about 10,000 years ago.

In the Vedic view, cosmic intelligence is the basis of all life. This places a greater emphasis on the evolution of consciousness than that of mere outer forms. What we see in nature is but a reflection of a deeper evolution of mind and consciousness that is a universal potential, not just a chance happening on Earth.

Consciousness pervades the entire universe, animate and inanimate. In living things, as per the limitations of body and mind, that consciousness has the capacity of feeling in the plant kingdom, and has an additional capacity of sensation in the animal kingdom. With human beings it has a power of intelligence through which the very creature can realize its oneness with God or the universal consciousness. That is the real goal of life in the Vedic sense.[5]

Natural History and the New View of Ancient India

HISTORY AS PART OF NATURAL HISTORY

This book is unique in that it brings in not only a spiritual perspective, but also one of natural history. Natural history includes the older history of our species before what we could call civilization was invented, as well as our interaction with the natural environment and its development over time.

Most history books today overlook the natural history of our species, which goes back tens of thousands of years before recorded history. This can have misleading consequences, particularly relative to the origins of civilization that depended upon earlier advances in agriculture, language and social interaction in the prehistoric era.

History books similarly ignore the importance of the natural environment as the prime factor in shaping culture and look upon political or economic factors as more significant. Yet floods, droughts and other natural calamities are usually more significant for beginning, ending or radically altering civilizations than simply internal social struggles.

According to our approach here, culture and civilization are primarily the human response to the natural environment and its changes; history is the record of this response. What we call history is but a phase in the natural history of our species and its greater development. Such a more 'ecological approach' to history is necessary in the current ecological age when we are again recognizing the importance of nature in shaping who we are. Human beings are part of the planet and cannot be looked upon as a species existing in isolation. Our activities affect and alter our ecosystems in ways that determine what our culture will be and how long it is likely to endure. This means that the natural history of India is the best context in which to start our examination of the human history of the region.

The natural history of India, meanwhile, is most closely related to that of Greater India, which has a similar pattern of mountains and monsoons in a tropical region. Therefore, one of the most significant consequences of this orientation to India's natural history takes us away from the focus on Central and West Asia as the basis of Indian civilization that has for too long dominated the discourse. It directs us to Greater India.[6] This has particularly important consequences relative to the natural history of both regions over the past more than 10,000 years, as we will demonstrate.

INDIA IN ITS NATURAL ENVIRONMENT: MATRI BHOOMI

Human beings and their culture arise out of the land like other species. They are part of their natural environment to which they must adapt in order to survive. Different cultures naturally reflect the circumstances of their geographical regions, climates and ecosystems. This is more important the further back in time we go and the more we look outside of urban environments, but even these are not above this law. To understand human history, we must look to natural history, particularly for ancient cultures that were much closer to the land than we are today. This begins with the facts of geography.

The motherland or Matri Bhoomi is the first guru of the people, one might say, just as the mother is the first guru of the child. The motherland of India is not only a great teacher but also a great provider for all aspects of life and humanity, holding a spiritual as well as material abundance for her children.

Mother India is not just a cultural and spiritual formulation but also a geographical reality, a unique formation of nature. With the highest mountains in the world and perhaps the greatest set of rivers, the land of India has shaped its people and its culture probably more than anything else has. This large tropical and subtropical subcontinent comes under the influence of the same natural forces of climate and geography, giving rise to similar responses from the people inhabiting the region.

India is a vast subcontinent located between the great mountain range of the Himalayas and the sea. It is a region defined by its special geography, which strongly insulates it from outside influences. The northern mountains are effective boundaries and remain almost impassable even today. The mountains to the west are part of a large desert region that serves to effectively block any easy access from that direction as well. The mountains of the east lead to successive ranges and almost impenetrable jungles in some of the wettest regions on Earth.

India's greatest access has always been by sea. From the west and into the Arabian Sea, India has a natural maritime route to the Persian Gulf, Arabia and the Red Sea. To the east through the Bay of Bengal it has an access to Greater India, Malaysia and Indonesia. Yet the southern and Eastern routes are much easier to travel because they lead to well-watered regions, while the Western sea routes cross extensive desert coastlines.[7]

The easy maritime access to the southeast is why in historical times Indian civilization naturally spread by sea to Malaysia, Indochina and Indonesia, following the course of the rivers and coastlines. India's geography and ecology provide the basis for its unique culture that has sustained itself through the millennia and also influenced the cultures around it which did have such an access to arable land

and vast rivers.

It is a fact of history, growing out of the natural environment and geography, that through most of its history India has been a maritime nation, depending upon a network of travel and trade on large rivers into the sea.[8]

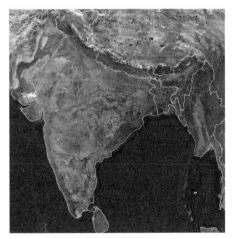

Figure 2: Present day India and South Asia

North India forms a vast plain defined by a series of great Himalayan rivers from the Indus in the west to the Brahmaputra in the east. These rivers provide an agricultural potential unparalleled in the rest of the world. While the civilization of ancient Egypt rested upon one great river, the Nile, and that of Mesopotamia on two great rivers, the Tigris and the Euphrates, ancient India had over a dozen such rivers and in a wetter and warmer subtropical climate. These great rivers of North India lead into the ocean either by the Arabian Sea or the Bay of Bengal and would naturally have led the culture towards maritime travel as well.

South India forms a plateau but also has its great rivers like the Narmada,

Krishna, Kaveri and Godavari that draw their waters from the heavy monsoon rains. The coastal regions are particularly well watered because the western and the eastern mountain ranges trap the rain-bearing monsoon winds. As a relatively small peninsula with oceans on both sides, its geography similarly creates a compelling connection to the ocean. Even connections to North India were often easier by sea than by land routes from South India.

India is blessed with probably the best agricultural region in the world. Though densely populated, even today its population is less dense than the United States when measured in terms of arable land. Its unique subtropical mountain, river and maritime ecosystem has allowed it to develop greater populations than Europe and the Middle East combined and made it a fertile ground for cultural growth.[9] Not surprisingly, ancient India's accounts of history and geography emphasize this great land with the Himalayas in the north, extending down to the sea, finding that to be a world in its own right and so are not much concerned with outside regions.[10]

The greater geographical region in which India is located is dominated by two major natural forces: the tropical (and subtropical) climate and the seasonal monsoon rains. The countries of Greater India come under the same influences, depending upon rivers that flow from their northern mountains that are extensions of the Himalayas. In terms of climate and natural history, India shares more with Greater India than with West Asia, Central Asia or Europe. This is reflected in the close connections between India and Greater India that go back tens of thousand of years. These run the gamut of the natural world including climate, flora and fauna and the people inhabiting the region.

We cannot, therefore, separate human achievements from the region's natural history. We must look for interpretations and explanations that connect the rhythm of nature with the progress (or decline) of civilizations. Our ancients understood this well when they sought to harmonize their lives with nature. They saw the divine manifesting everything in nature, living and non-living – from the grandest to the most humble. As a seer in the Yajur Veda puts it:

Iśāvasyamidam sarvam, yatkiñcit jagatyām jagat.

"All this universe is pervaded by the Lord, whatsoever moving thing there is in this moving world."[11]

The ideals of nature worship that we see in Vedic texts and in other ancient scriptures and teachings reflect a deeper connection with the Divine Spirit pervading nature. It is not at all a primitive, but a progressive, all-comprehensive understanding of life. The truth of interconnectedness and interdependency, and the need of co-existence – that the human being is a part of nature and cannot survive without it – are hidden in these rituals. It reflects a deeper inner and an ecological vision, such as we are only just now beginning to discover and appreciate in this modern, ecological age.

INDIA AND GREATER INDIA: ICE AGE AND BEYOND

The natural history of our species is dominated by one very significant natural event over the last fifteen thousand years. This is the end of the last Ice Age. The end of the Ice Age radically changed climates worldwide, submerged extensive coastal regions and caused extensive migrations of people. Its effects on India and Greater India were particularly important, devastating and transforming to the entire environment. These events form the basis of any real examination of the history of the region or of the history of humanity as a whole.

India's links with Greater India were even closer ten thousand years ago and earlier during the Ice Age period when the whole region – from peninsular India to Indonesia – formed at various times either a single landmass or a massive archipelago of islands and peninsulas separated by relatively shallow, easy to cross sea-lanes. This created a vast landmass known as 'Sunda Land'. Large areas of Sunda Land along with a substantial strip of the Indian coast were submerged by rising sea levels when the last Ice Age ended. This has to be the natural background from which to begin any study of the history and culture of the Indian people. Their history cannot be set apart from these natural connections with Greater India and its populations. Nor can we ignore the impact of the cataclysms on the inhabitants of the region.

Sunda Land and South India, especially the coastal regions, were the most favourable places for populations. Since they both had abundant heat and moisture, throughout the Ice Age period, when much of the northern hemisphere was cold, arid and inhospitable. This may be reflected in South Indian recollections of Kanya Kumari, a larger Pacific continent to the South, and to Vedic references to the sea and early maritime cultures. It is also why the peoples of India and regions referred to as Greater India are genetically older and more diverse than those of Europe and West Asia. This is because these regions constitute a single natural zone united by geography, climate and natural history. In view of this unity, which is of untold antiquity and is also reflected in the history and culture of the region, it is properly called Greater India. Modern terms like Indo-China and Indonesia are no more than recognitions of this historical fact.

When sea levels rose, it was these best habitable lands that were lost, triggering migrations to the interior and the north. This was probably the greatest and most consequential migration in human history that set in motion most of the cultures and civilizational changes that came later. It holds one of the keys to understanding the region's prehistory along with its chronology.

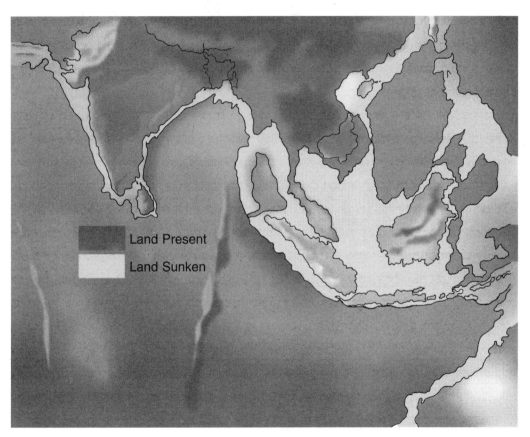

Figure 3: Ice Age map of Greater India including the submerged Sunda Land

Figure 4: Ice Age maps showing land connections (left) and Sunda Land (right) during the Ice Age

NATURAL HISTORY AND GENETICS

In recent decades, there have been significant advances in our knowledge of our past thanks to new techniques based on genetic mapping. As this is a very new discipline, still learning to define itself and its capacities, there remains a good deal of controversy but this much seems to be reasonably certain: our ancestors or *Homo sapiens* originated in Africa around 150,000 years ago. A small group eventually left Africa some 80,000 years ago and settled along the coast of South

Asia from which they gradually spread out to colonize different parts of the world. All non-Africans in the world today are descended from a small group of South Asians living south of a line from Yemen to the Himalayas, especially from those along the Indian coast.[12] *This means that after Africa, India is the second homeland of our human species.*

This 'founder group', from which all non-Africans are descended, barely survived the fallout from a volcanic eruption in Sumatra known as the 'Toba Explosion', 74,000 years ago. The Toba Explosion was the greatest catastrophe ever to hit humanity. It almost put an end to non-African human populations, but a core group survived in India, which became the jumping off point for the ultimate colonization of the world.[13] This means that the Indian population is largely indigenous from the earliest times of the Toba Explosion and is not the result of recent migrations as held by many historians and anthropologists.[14]

The Europeans were among the descendents from these early South Asians, possibly as recently as 40,000 years ago. *South Asia, India in particular, was the jumping off point for the colonization of East Asia, Greater India, Australia and ultimately the Americas.*

The data for this is summarized by Luigi Luca Cavalli-Sforza, arguably the world's foremost population geneticist, and his colleagues, in the following words:

> Results show that Indian tribal and caste populations derive largely from the same genetic heritage of Pleistocene southern and Western Asians *and have received limited gene flow from external regions since the Holocene.* The phylogeography [neighboring branches] of the primal mtDNA and Y-chromosome founders suggests that these southern Asian Pleistocene coastal settlers from Africa would have provided the inocula for the subsequent differentiation of the distinctive Eastern and Western Eurasian gene pools. (Italics added.)[15]

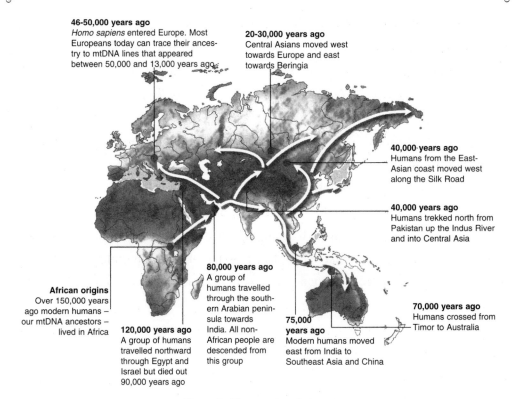

46-50,000 years ago
Homo sapiens entered Europe. Most Europeans today can trace their ancestry to mtDNA lines that appeared between 50,000 and 13,000 years ago.

20-30,000 years ago
Central Asians moved west towards Europe and east towards Beringia

40,000 years ago
Humans from the East-Asian coast moved west along the Silk Road

40,000 years ago
Humans trekked north from Pakistan up the Indus River and into Central Asia

African origins
Over 150,000 years ago modern humans – our mtDNA ancestors – lived in Africa

120,000 years ago
A group of humans travelled northward through Egypt and Israel but died out 90,000 years ago

80,000 years ago
A group of humans travelled through the southern Arabian peninsula towards India. All non-African people are descended from this group

75,000 years ago
Modern humans moved east from India to Southeast Asia and China

70,000 years ago
Humans crossed from Timor to Australia

Figure 5: Human migration map

Put in non-technical language, it means that the Indian population and all its varied constituents, however defined – upper castes, lower castes, tribals (or so-called indigenous peoples), Dravidians and so forth – are all mainly of indigenous origin, and the contribution of immigrants (gene flow) is negligible. This is a major blow to the many invasion-migration theories that continue to dominate historical discourse in India. In particular, the various theories about Aryans and non-Aryans have no scientific basis whatsoever. In fact, such genetic information calls into question the entire concept of race as a primary factor for explaining the movements of people in ancient history.

Seen against this background, it is natural that the human inhabitants of India and Greater India, like the climate and its flora and fauna, should remain closely related. This is precisely what recent biological studies have also revealed. And this connection goes back at least 50,000 years. It is the descendants of these early humans who created both Indian and Greater Indian civilizations — art, archaeology and literature. Their influence also spread north and west.

This means that contrary to older views that India was mainly populated from the outside in historical times, India has actually been a major source of the world's populations going back many tens of thousands of years, of which the movement at the end of the last Ice Age was the largest and the most important.

Summary: Science and the cosmic spirit

What we call history is, to a great extent, an artificial line, defining people as either civilized or uncivilized based upon markers like writing, urban development or the use of metals that may not be crucial to the real character of people. It is unlikely that earlier humanity was any less human or any less sensitive than we are, even if they did not build cities like we do. So-called primitive peoples often produced art and literature far superior than what is being produced today.

It is also a well known fact of history that so-called primitive people in the colonial era, like the Native Americans, were often more honest, kind and truthful than their European conquerors, who never honoured a single treaty with them. Scientifically speaking, the yogi in a cave and the caveman are indistinguishable to the urban markers of modern civilization, though they are radically different relative to the evolution of consciousness.

In this regard, Hindu records through the Vedas and Purans suggest that human civilization – or at least some sort of advanced culture capable of spiritual development – has been going on much longer than our recorded history. These texts connect human history with longer natural and cosmic cycles, and current humanity with earlier humanities of tens of thousands of years ago.

It has also been the view of many spiritual thinkers worldwide that there were earlier humanities that underwent their own cultural developments, though not necessarily in a technological manner. The ancient Greeks, Egyptians and Babylonians firmly believed this. We are only now beginning to suspect these possibilities. What was previously regarded as the beginning of history around 3000 BCE (5000 BP) is now being seen as part of a longer natural history, with culture, agriculture and language being much older.

The Vedas project a 'Yuga' theory of historical and cosmic development, the idea of periodic cycles of humanity and of nature, broken by great natural catastrophes. This fits in well with current scientific theories about natural history through the Ice Ages and warm periods like the one we are living in today. There are two cycles of 41,000 years and 24,000 years duration that overlap the 100,000-year Ice Age cycle, which are the main cycles of natural history scientists are looking at relative to early humanity. These are characterized by the position of the Earth's axis relative to the Sun, and therefore the amount of energy that the Earth receives. Though the exact relationships are not known, these cycles have a bearing on the world's climate and a profound effect on the life of all species. The Vedic Yuga cycle of 24,000 years reflects similar time frames.

The idea of earlier Manus and earlier *kalpas,* or world-ages, such as we find in the Puranic literature, may reflect memories of these earlier phases of mankind prior to what our current culture recognizes as history. This Hindu connection to prehistoric eras of the human species may be responsible for the Hindu idea of an eternal tradition of truth (Sanatan Dharma). It extends to the Hindu view of the universe, which is defined according to longer natural cycles of *yugas* extending into the age of the universe itself and a recognition that our current universe is only one of many that exists throughout the endless expanse of time and space.

From the standpoint of modern science, this 'Hindu view of time' better reflects the movement of natural history (and cosmology) that is marked by cycles and cataclysms over long periods of time. It stands in stark contrast to Western historical models that follow a linear and progressive model of history, generally focussed on events of the last five thousand years, if not the last five hundred. These place human history apart from nature's cycles and often opposed to them as well.

Such linear time models extend to Western politics and religion. The Western mind then interprets history according to its own linear models, and ignores the role of natural history and its cycles that was the real time frame in which ancient people actually lived.

As we move into an ecological age, we must once more respect natural history and natural time cycles. This will take the modern mind back in the direction of the Hindu view of time and the Hindu approach to history that has always based itself on such natural time cycles and a regard for the much greater antiquity of the human species. It also accommodates new discoveries in fields as diverse as natural history, genetics and cosmology.

The Aryan Fantasy

'ARYAN'

No single aspect of ancient Indian history has so dominated historical discourse as the so-called 'Aryan problem'. In the nineteenth century, European scholars, new to the study of India, proposed an 'Aryan invasion' that was supposed to have brought the Vedic civilization and the 'Aryan' language (Sanskrit) to India from the Aryan west. The theory led to the illusory idea of an Aryan race, generally blond and blue-eyed which fuelled a pathological attempt to recreate an Aryan nation years later in, of all places, Germany!

Even archaeology has not escaped the Aryan obsession, with scholars claiming that the Harappan civilization was non-Aryan, destroyed by the invading Aryans. Mortimer Wheeler, one of the early Harappan archaeologists, went so far as to try to read an Aryan massacre into skeletal remains he found at Mohenjodaro, which he highlighted with great drama and which has entered into many textbooks, still used to the present day. Though later archaeology disproved Wheeler's finding as a case of imagination gone wild, showing that the skeletons showed no evidence of violent deaths, and no Harappan sites have ever been found that were destroyed by outside invaders, archaeologists still talk about the incoming Aryans, hoping to find them eventually, somewhere! Meanwhile the depiction of the Aryans has retreated from massive destructive hordes to small groups of undetectable migrants, hoping to preserve the theory even if no evidence in favour of it can be found. The Aryan idea appears more like an article of faith for Western historians than anything inherent in the facts coming out of India. What is the reality?

In the whole of the Rig Veda, consisting of ten books and more than a thousand hymns, the word 'Arya' appears fewer than forty times. It may occur as many times in a few pages of a modern European work like Hitler's *Mein Kampf*, where there is no doubt about its racial meaning. As a result, any modern book or even discussion on the 'Aryan problem' is more likely to be a commentary on recent European thought on the Aryans than on anything really relevant to the ancient India of many thousands of years ago.

This use of the term Aryan can be compared with the fear of the Swastika as a symbol of racism and hatred, with which it is often falsely combined. The Swastika is an old Vedic symbol of good fortune, found in the oldest archaeological sites in India.[16] It is a solar symbol of enlightenment that the Buddhists and Jains also adopted. Other than the gross misuse by the Nazis, the Swastika — more popularly the Svasti — has been used as a symbol of goodwill and well-being all over the world. Not only Indians and other Asians, but also Romans and even some Native American tribes have used the Swastika as such a symbol. Except for a fleeting period of Nazi misuse, the Swastika has been a universal symbol of peace and prosperity.

The Rig Veda and all of Sanskrit literature that followed never refer to Aryans in this modern sense of the word. Aryan was an important title of respect, roughly comparable to the English word 'sir' or 'gentleman'. It was used to symbolize nobility and refinement of behaviour and character, not a pattern of bias and prejudice to which it has been turned into by modern writers! The ancient Sanskrit lexicon *Amarakosha* identifies it as a synonym for honourable or praiseworthy conduct.

There is no reference to any 'Aryan' type, race or tribe as a term of ethnicity in Sanskrit literature. There is only Aryan as a certain type of high culture or lofty code of conduct. Even the Buddha called his religion 'Arya Dharma' in this manner. We cannot imagine Aryans conquered ancient India and took over all titles of respect in the country, any more than we can imagine that a tribe of Englishmen named 'sir' took over all the main positions of power in England!

The Vedic deities or *devas* were regarded as forces of light and their enemies were regarded as forces of darkness, just as was the case for many ancient solar religions, from America and Egypt to Europe and India. But this was not meant as a racial statement, but just the natural symbolizm of light and darkness.

Yet the truth is that after two hundred years and many books on the subject of the Aryans, scholars are still unclear what the Aryan identity is. At first the Aryans were supposed to be a race distinguished by physical traits like white skin, blond hair and blue eyes, but given the lack of any evidence for such types in India or Iran, countries of the most ancient Aryan cultures, this has largely been given up. Other scholars have gone so far as to identify Aryan as Caucasian, though there are many Caucasian groups that have darker skin and many others who do not speak so-called Aryan languages. Scientists, too, have no use for the 'Aryan race'. As far back as 1939, Julian Huxley, one of the great biologists of the 20th century, dismissed it as part of "political and propagandist" literature.

Genetics is a new science that is adding important new information about human origins, but even with it some initial data has been distorted by the Aryan obsession. A recent study conducted by Bamshad et al. at the University of Utah claims to have found evidence of Western, possible Indo-European or Aryan peoples in the DNA of some South Indian peoples (actually too small a group to prove the point). Their claims that they have identified genes relating to tribes and even castes (and sometimes language!) make no scientific sense. The study resembles Wheeler's imaginary massacre at Mohenjodaro. This genetic study has similarly been discredited by more important thinkers in the field. Eminent geneticists like L. Cavalli-Sforza and Stephen Oppenheimer have rejected it.[17] According to them, the M17 genetic marker, which is supposed to distinguish the 'Caucasian' type, occurs with the highest frequency and diversity in India, showing that among its carriers, the Indian population is the oldest.

Archaeologically speaking, the search for Aryan skeletons in India has not come up with anything either. There are to date no ruins, remains, encampments or settlements of any invading Aryans that anyone has ever been able to show or prove to have existed apart from indigenous developments.

Sensitive to the disrepute that race theories have fallen into, some scholars hold on to the Aryan term but as referring to a linguistic group. This began with the German-born Indologist Max Müller, one of the main proponents of Aryanism, who made a celebrated switch from Aryan as race to Aryan as language. Yet the vast body of Indian literature on linguistics, the richest in the world going back to Yaska, Panini and Vedic texts, knows nothing of any Aryan language as the dialect of a particular group of people. When used relative to language, Aryan refers to noble or cultured speech, like well-educated individuals who speak good Sanskrit, similar to people speaking good English versus those speaking common or vulgar forms. This does not mean that those speaking unrefined speech are speaking a different language or are of a different ethnicity!

The 'Aryan nation' of Aryan racial purity was the battle cry of German nationalists, not ancient Indians. To look at ancient Sanskrit terms in light of their modern

European redefinitions cannot lead us anywhere in understanding the ancient world, however much political passion it may arouse.

All this means that the 'Aryan problem' is mainly a non-problem – an aberration of wrong history and inaccurate semantics. It has been kept alive by certain historians, who have taken the Sanskrit term to mean what they would like it to. According to its advocates, because of linguistic similarities with languages of Europe and Central Asia, the Vedic language and literature must be of non-Indian origin, and so must have been brought in by a different ethnic group, whom they propose was the invading or migrating Aryans. This is proved not by any evidence of these incoming Aryans, but by the linguistic requirements of modern theories.

In other words, certain scholars have invented the Aryans as a people to give justification to their own theories. The idea of the invading Aryans was proposed even before any major archaeological finds relative to ancient India were made, and continued long after archaeology contradicted the invasion idea. It has ignored or distorted those finds that came later. Aryans are needed because without them there can be no Aryan invasion (or migration) needed to justify certain linguistic theories. *In the face of all this it is best to ignore labels and look simply at the record of the people who lived in India and created her unique civilizations.*

THE ARYAN INVASION

When we open a history book used in our schools today, we find that it invariably begins with a description of the Indus Valley Civilization. It usually starts off with an account of the discovery of the two major sites Harappa and Mohenjodaro, followed by a brief description of what was found there. We will also be told how this civilization went into decline and finally disappeared by 1500 BCE (3500 BP). The main cause of this disappearance, the reader is then informed, was the invasion of India by nomadic tribes from Central Asia called the Aryans. According to this account, these invading Aryans, who are said to have entered India through the passes in the northwest, fought and overcame the inhabitants of the Indus Valley and established themselves over much of North India. They are then said to have composed their literature, the most important of which is the Rig Veda. The history of India begins in earnest with the records of the Aryans following their invasion. This in essence is the account of ancient history found not only in school books, but also in such authoritative sources as the *Encyclopaedia Britannica*.

The modern science of molecular genetics has demolished the whole notion of the Aryans. Archaeology also has disproved the idea of an Aryan invasion. In addition to political and racial ideas that were given a linguistic garb, some religious beliefs also played a part in creating the Aryan Invasion Theory. In 19th century Europe many students were taught the Biblical superstition that the world was created in its present form with all its life forms on 23 October 4004 BCE. European scholars steeped in this belief, could not accept that Indian history and civilization went much further back in time. So they distorted and misinterpreted records to fit their own limited worldview.

In recent years, recognizing that the Aryan Invasion Theory has been disproved, some scholars are proposing something they are calling the Aryan Migration Theory. This, too, is no more valid. All the old contradictions remain and some new ones arise as well. We reject both for the same reasons.

ARYAN AND CASTE

Unfortunately, these proposed Vedic Aryan hordes have been portrayed by Western historians as primitive Nazis bringing racial oppression into ancient India. These mythical Aryan invaders have been attributed with caste oppression and all other Indian social evils. Yet such scholars fail to note that the type of class and clan society we find in the Vedas is very much like what existed throughout the ancient world, continues in tribal societies everywhere, and persists in some forms in modern societies as well. It is not an Aryan invention.

The rule was the same in most ancient cultures; chieftains and priests formed a special group at the top. The common people were divided into merchants, farmers and servants, with some populations on the outside of the social order kept in the distance. Such a division does not reflect any single political or religious ideology, much less a particular ethnicity, but just the practicalities of organizing society in the pre-technological and largely non-urban world (even in the Harappan area with its numerous urban sites the great majority of people lived in villages).

There is no need to invent the Aryans to bring in the caste system, any more than to bring in the Sanskrit language. The pride of birth is high and often an important source of status in all cultures and societies. It does not require invaders to produce it. Such abuse of status is a common human problem, which continues today in various forms. It cannot simply be used to blame some mythical Aryans of thousands of years ago.

Yet today, even when most Western historians have rejected the scenario of the pillaging Aryan hordes, they are doing very little to correct the distortions caused by it, often allowing these wrong accounts to continue in old textbooks without revision.

They have thereby allowed the anti-Hindu or anti-Vedic sentiments generated by such ideas to go on without any serious challenge. Such characterizations border on racism and breed conflict and misunderstanding. *It is necessary to remove these Aryan distortions for a correct view of ancient India. That is part of our purpose in writing this book.*

The Issue of Language

According to many spiritual traditions, East and West, in the beginning was the Word. This is true both of cosmic creation and of human history. Speech is the basis of all human culture. In the Vedic view, the faculty that most defines the human beings is speech, the essence of which is OM, the cosmic sound that creates the entire universe through its vibratory power.

The key to the origins of civilization and high thinking in humanity is linked to the development of speech. Other markers of civilization like writing and urban constructions are secondary and became possible only because of the spoken word. Yet speech arose much earlier in history than urban civilization, and it is likely that some form of speech has been with modern humans since our origins a hundred thousand years ago or more. Some societies that have not used writing have also had a high degree of verbal skills through oral poetry and story traditions.

The study of the ancient world must consider the development of ancient languages and, when existent, their literary records. In this regard, India has left us the greatest literature of the ancient world, the Vedic, and the greatest language, Sanskrit. This in itself tells us a lot about the importance of Indian civilization, its continuity and its antiquity. Only a great culture could produce and preserve such a language that has endured when all other great ancient languages have fallen into extinction.

Yet language records, by which we mean written texts, go back only some 5000 years, and even then only in fragments. This means that we cannot reduce ancient languages and the development of human speech to the available written records, however useful these might be. Efforts to explain the current languages of India have been based upon proposed migrations of people over the last three or four thousand years only. Now we can see that these follow too short a time frame to account for cultural developments and connections in the region, which were already well in place long before this period.

THE PROBLEM OF LINGUISTICS

Our modern view of the ancient world is coloured by another modern discipline apart from archaeology. This is linguistics, or the comparative study of languages. Linguistics attempts to recreate postulated ancient languages. It then tries to use these creations to recover the history and the movements of people as if language was the primary determinative factor in how or why people migrated. This is sometimes called historical linguistics.

However, we must remember that linguistics is not a hard science like genetics nor based on technical evidence like archaeology. There is no genetic material in the human being that can be identified with particular languages or language families. There is, for example, no Indo-European gene or Dravidian gene or Sanskrit gene!

Linguistics reflects certain assumptions about language and its development that linguists have today. The assumption that ancient people viewed and developed their languages many thousands of years ago, the way we theorize they did cannot be accepted as scientifically proven. As we shall soon discover, science casts serious doubt on it.

For these reasons, we cannot treat linguistics as a primary source for determining what occurred in the ancient world. It may be of secondary value, if at all, for refining correlations based on more solid forms of evidence.

INDO-EUROPEAN LANGUAGES

The discovery of connections between Sanskrit and many languages of Europe, the Middle East and Central Asia, caused nineteenth century scholars to posit an 'Indo-European' family of languages. Such ancient languages as Latin, Greek, Iranian and Sanskrit have many affinities as do later languages in the Germanic, Slavic, Baltic and others. This led them to posit some original Proto-Indo-European language behind all these from which these different languages arose as branches.

Based on this idea, scholars proposed an original homeland of this Proto-Indo-European group somewhere in Central Asia as a kind of common point of dispersion in different directions. They also proposed that the Vedic language and culture arose as a result of migrations from this region. In addition, many tried to relate this original linguistic group with some sort of racial identity or ethnicity, not surprisingly European Caucasoid! The term 'Aryan language' is an invention of Western scholars used to mean such Indo-European languages – historical and reconstructed.

Yet the fact that Indo-European languages are related in some ways is no proof that they evolved from a single language, much less the place or time when that might have occurred. The so-called Indo-European languages have connections with non-Indo-European languages as well. The similarities between Indo-European languages can be explained in other ways than from a migration into India, for which there is no evidence. For example, there could be movements out of India or other forms of cultural diffusion.

The division of languages into families is not watertight. Vedic Sanskrit has affinities with the Dravidian and Munda languages of India also. These connections extend to common loan words and common grammatical formations even for languages that might be classified as otherwise belonging to different language families. There appears to be no easy way of fitting languages into separate families.

Our view is that just as India has maintained a continuity of peoples and cultures within its geographical zone, the same is true of its languages. A region that could develop great languages like Sanskrit and Tamil cannot be held deficient as far as language is concerned. Indeed, Vedic grammar and linguistics as reflected in Panini and other more ancient texts is the most sophisticated in the world. The creative genius of India has long gone into language, grammar, metrics, etymology, mantra and other language studies, both scientific and spiritual. It is hardly a linguistic vacuum zone, only borrowing its languages from the outside, as some linguists propose. As with genetics, so with languages. The greatest diversity and the highest antiquity of Sanskrit and its derivatives are found in India. This is strong evidence that Sanskrit was born in India.

LANGUAGE AND NATURAL HISTORY

A major problem with migration theories of languages – which include the idea that the original Sanskrit speakers migrated to India sometime after 1500 BCE (3500 BP) – is that it was rather late in the ancient period in which populations, civilizations, customs and languages were already well established.

The main migration of peoples and of languages would have been from the south and east at the end of the Ice Age. This was a consequence of natural history and the climatic upheavals that took place at the time. It was at this time that disruptions owing to climate changes would have created the maximum necessity for such movements of people. Yet if post-Ice Age events were the main impetus behind the development of both languages and cultures, it would make most of the languages of the world older than current estimates.

At best, the Indo-European group of languages reflects older cultural connections that began with these movements of peoples at the end of the Ice Age. The dominance of so-called Indo-European civilizations like India, Iran, Greece and Rome aided in the continuity of such linguistic groups, but is not their origin.

In this regard it is helpful to look at what current science has to say about the language problem. Recent studies in the human genome suggest that some mutations in a gene called *FOXP2* may have triggered the uniquely human capacity for speech and therefore language. Dates are uncertain, but all humans inhabiting the world today – traceable to an exodus from Africa perhaps 90,000 years ago – possess this capacity. Hence it is reasonable to suppose that the necessary mutations in speech production, hearing and cognition (comprehension) must have taken place 100,000 years ago at the least.[18]

Chronology is not the only problem with linguistics as a tool in history. Linguistic methods fail scientific tests also. As published in *Mathematics in the Archaelogical and Historical Sciences,* when Kruksal, Dyen and Black applied statistical tests to the languages that make up the Indo-European family, they found results that contradicted the most basic assumption of linguists – that they form a language family. The most important member is of course Sanskrit, but their analysis threw up a major contradiction: Indian and Iranian languages failed the grouping test! This is a bombshell, for according to Indo-European linguistics, Indo-Iranian is the lynchpin of the whole discipline, but the one quantitative test that was applied to the hypothesis discredited it.[19]

Struck by this, Cavalli-Sforza highlighted that the Kruksal, Dyen and Black study "...found no similarity at all between Italic and Celtic languages, nor between Indian and Iranian ones... The non-identification of an Indo-Iranian group by Dyen, et al. is the major departure from the conclusions accepted by the majority of traditional linguists."[20] In other words, much of what was regarded as solid fact in linguistics remains highly questionable, if not outright wrong.

The point to note here is that the tests do not deny that Sanskrit and ancient Iranian (Avestan) are related. They question the methodology used in deriving language families, which is the main tool of comparative linguistics. Since comparative linguistics is the basis of various migration theories, including the Aryan invasion (or migration) theory, it is hardly surprising that both comparative linguistics and invasion-migration theories should have fallen victims to rigorous scientific analysis. Both now stand discredited for the same reason: they are unscientific.

Aryan–Dravidian Fiction

Besides the effort to define the Aryans as a linguistic group associated with a certain ethnic type, a similar effort has been made relative to the Dravidians, even though the ancient Dravidian kings also called themselves Arya as a title of respect! (No known ruling dynasty in South India ever called itself 'Dravidian' as apart from the Aryan.) Modern genetics shows that there is no more a Dravidian race than there is an Aryan race. The populations of India are largely indigenous and interrelated, including north and south, though regional variations naturally exist in such a large subcontinent.

Dravidian as a term in Indian literature refers to the people of peninsular India, specifically the Pancha Dravida or five Dravidian regions. These are Gujarat, Maharashtra, Karnataka, Tamil Nadu and Andhra Pradesh. It indicates mainly the region of South India as a geographical entity. It never referred to a cultural divide, but does reflect certain cultural variations. Dravidian peoples also follow an Indian civilization whose principles and practices are in harmony with those used in the rest of India since ancient times, but with some local variations.

Yet strangely, those who require an Aryan invasion or migration to explain the existence of Indo-European languages in India require a similar Dravidian migration to explain the existence of Dravidian languages in India. Some scholars suggest this proposed Dravidian invasion occurs after (sometimes before) their proposed Aryan invasion. The idea goes back to Bishop Caldwell who first invented the Aryan-Dravidian divide and regarded the Dravidians as a Scythian people from Central Asia.[21] This idea is based on the supposed affinities between Dravidian and Central Asian languages, just as the Aryan invasion is based on affinities between Sanskrit and Central Asian languages.

Such scholars cannot find much by way of any indigenous languages in India, though clearly there were enough people to create and sustain their own language traditions! In light of both the older origin for languages and the long existence of the Indian populations, we cannot reduce the history of the region to racial and linguistic labels and stereotypes like 'Aryans' or 'Dravidians'. Such vaguely defined groups are largely modern constructs and reflect modern concerns more than ancient realities. They are based on now antiquated linguistic and ethnic theories following a reduced chronology of the last several thousand years that is too short to explain the developments in the region.

Relative to North and South India, the natural history shows a movement of people and culture from the south to the north at the end of the Ice Age. One result of this was the development of a new civilization in the Sarasvati River region of North India after 8000 BCE (10,000 BP). Yet southern cultures continued and interacted with the Vedic Sarasvati culture, which was originally an offshoot of those in the south. This means that claims of earlier cultures in South India must be taken seriously as well.

Curiously, the greatest of the Rig Vedic seers, Vasishtha, is portrayed as the younger brother of Agatsya, the dominant seer for South India and Greater India and for Tamil Nadu. Agatsya himself has twenty-five hymns in the Rig Veda. So it is likely that proto-Vedic and proto-Tamilian culture were closely related, if not sharing a common origin. Peoples of the south, like the Turvashas and the Yadus, are also highly praised in the Rig Veda, even though the peoples of North India like the Purus are given the greatest importance.

From Natural History to Recorded History

THE SHIFT TO THE SARASVATI RIVER AND THE VEDIC AGE

Most of us can remember the accounts of history that we found as children in our school textbooks, showing the Near East as the 'Cradle of Civilization', with writing and urban development beginning in Sumeria about 5000 years ago. This type of history arose during the period of European colonializm and owed much of its orientation to it. The same period saw the beginnings of archaeology as a discipline.

However, what is now becoming clear today is that these accounts may not be as definitive as first thought. Neither the time of the beginning of civilization nor its location is as clear as previously considered. We need not treat these propositions as scientific facts but as the conjecture of a certain era that may require major revision over time. This very idea of history and its time frames seems progressively out of harmony with a universe defined by consciousness, as modern physics is now showing it to be.

Nineteenth century European scholars naturally looked to the regions close to their homelands. They emphasized their own ancient literary records from Greek sources and the Bible, which derived their civilizations mainly from ancient Egypt and Mesopotamia. Archaeologists focussed their work in the same areas, which, as desert regions, were also particularly good for preserving ruins. Since this brought them to the river valleys of the Nile and the Tigris-Euphrates delta, it also became an article of faith among them that human civilization began in the river valleys of the Near East.

Scholars then went on to create historical models based on this belief. They took the dates of what they had discovered with their new disciplines as the date for the birth of civilization itself, which gave an antiquity of about 5000 years for human culture. This occurred at a time in which it was thought the human species was not much older than that.[22] They looked at everything before this as prehistoric or primitive. Other regions like India and China, though long famous for large and ancient civilizations, were given little attention or scrutiny, as if they had little importance at all. Their ancient literature, which was no more religious or mythical than that of the Greeks or the Bible, was dismissed as largely without any historical basis at all.

Only after major archaeological finds were made in India in the early twentieth century was ancient India reluctantly brought into the picture, but even then it was never really integrated into the main movement of historical development as proposed by Western thinkers. Ancient India was treated more as a borrowing or even dead-end in the main development of world civilization through the West.

Origins: from Coastal Environments to River Valleys

However, when we look at the climatic conditions, we must recognize that the earliest human settlements were likely to have occurred in the tropics, particularly in coastal regions where environmental factors were much milder, especially during the long Ice Ages that have dominated the life of our species.[23] It was only centuries after the Ice Age ended that land-based settlements could evolve to the point they could support major populations. *This means that the river valley civilizations of Egypt, Mesopotamia and India (the Indus/Sarasvati Valley) represent a later phase of human settlement and culture, not the beginning.*

In order to truly understand the origins of civilization we must go back to an earlier maritime phase, the late Ice Age period in which populations were centred in tropical coastal areas, preceding these river civilizations by thousands of years. These sites are located not in Central Asia, Eurasia or Europe, but in the coastal regions of peninsular India and coastal regions from the east, particularly in the now submerged landmass of Sunda Land. *This maritime focus represents a major point of departure from current versions of Indian history.* [24]

TRANSITION TO AGRICULTURE: POST-ICE AGE PHENOMENON

The same nineteenth century focus on the Near East as the cradle of civilization attributed the region with the origin of agriculture, the main factor behind the later development of urban civilization. It is still widely held that agriculture began less than ten thousand years ago in the region of the 'Fertile Crescent', a belt stretching from the Nile valley in Egypt to the Tigris-Euphrates delta and beyond in Southwestern Asia. According to this view, it spans also "the crescent arches through the Levant and the Jordan valley through southeastern Turkey and across the Iranian highlands and northern Iraq."[25]

Yet 'fertile crescent' is itself a misnomer. Many regions of Asia possess much more fertile lands and a greater potential for agriculture, while the Fertile Crescent region is only the slightly wetter portion of what is essentially an arid region. There is no reason to assume that these wetter Asiatic regions could not develop agriculture and the evidence also supports it.

Agriculture actually first appears in Greater India by 10,000 BCE (12,000 BP) and is only noted in the Fertile Crescent more than a thousand years later.[26] And this is true even though little ground work has been done in Greater India exploring possible early agricultural sites (which if coastal are likely to be under water today).

Furthermore, during the crucial period just before the first signs of agriculture can be proved, which was during the late Ice Age period some ten to fifteen thousand years ago, the world was struck by the two cold periods — the Older and the Younger Dryas — and even the tropics came under severe drought. At that time the so-called Fertile Crescent would have been acutely short of water. Greater India was then even more favourably placed for the transition from plant gathering to the cultivation of domestic crops.

This means that agriculture probably arose first in Greater India and reached India from there. In this regard, we should note that the famous humped or Brahma bull (*Bos Indicus*), the mainstay of agriculture in India, is not descended from West Asian Aurochian cattle, which would make sense if India gained its agriculture from the West, but from the wild Asiatic one known as the Banteng (*Bos Banteng*), a close relative of the Indian bison or *gaur*. Studies show that the European cattle (Auroch) and the Indian are separated by an evolutionary distance of at least 600,000 years.

THE SHIFT TO NORTH INDIA

At the end of the last Ice Age, sea levels rose dramatically, four hundred feet in some areas. Vast coastal areas and the great landmass of Sunda Land went permanently under water and Indonesia became divided into various islands. Sri Lanka was separated from peninsular India. The Andaman and Nicobar Islands, once part of a peninsula of Greater India became small outposts in the sea.

Most of the best habitable lands of Greater India were submerged and their inhabitants were forced to move to the interior. The high temperatures melted the glaciers and gave abundant rainfall, bringing heat and water to previously dry, cold and inhospitable regions. The pull to new fertile areas inland was accelerated by the flooding in coastal homelands. Ancient humanity witnessed a planetary transformation unlike anything that we have seen in recorded history.

As the Ice Age ended, the Himalayan rivers began to flow with abundant waters. The monsoon extended northward and increased in intensity. The main populations in India shifted from the southern coasts to the northern rivers. The warmer temperatures and melting glaciers brought about a great renewal to North India, transforming its dry, cool region into a rich, moist and fertile set of great river valleys, of easy access to the peoples arriving from the south and the east.

Yet the Ice Age did not end in one single event. There were several periods of warming and cooling in the late Ice Age period (the Older and Younger Dryas – a prolonged cold, dry spell). North India became wetter and opened up for habitation during these late Ice Age warm periods, when Europe and Central Asia were still locked in glaciers. This means that populations from Greater India would have already begun moving out to the northwest during these late Ice Age warm periods. When they did so they would have first reached North India, which was accessible by both land and sea.

Once the Ice Age completely ended, populations from North India could have served as a staging ground for further migrations north and west. *This provides us a twofold migration from the southeast to the northwest: the first to northwest India, the second from there into Central Asia and Europe. If Greater India (including South India) was the origin of the main human migrations, North India was likely its main point of advance.*

The Sarasvati River

Yet at that early ancient period the river systems of North India would not be the same as they were later. The massive glacial flows in this relatively flat plain would have carved different streams than what we find today. Geology shows us that after the end of the Ice Age North India was dominated by a now dried river, flowing roughly parallel to the Indus but to the east of it, from the Himalayas to the Rann of Kachchh. Most ancient archaeological sites in India, both urban and pre-urban, are found along its banks.

Curiously, such a river is not only known to the ancient Vedic literature of India but is described in great detail as the very original homeland of the Vedic people and the cradle of Vedic civilization – the great Sarasvati River. This rediscovery of the Sarasvati River has revindicated the antiquity of Vedic literature in India, showing that Vedic texts were familiar with its geography and the river systems of over five thousand years ago.

Relative to the origins of agriculture in India, K.S. Valdiya, a researcher at the Jawaharlal Nehru Centre for Scientific Research, has written: "The discovery of burnt stubbles of cereal plants along with cutigents in the pollens, trapped in the sediments of the lakes Lunkaransar and Didwana in western Rajasthan, shows that the people of the Sarasvati domain had taken to agriculture in the early Holocene time (post-Ice Age). This is borne out from the charcoal that gives a date of 9400 to 8000 BP (7400 to 6000 BCE)." This shows the importance of the Sarasvati River from the very end of the Ice Age itself as a site of major habitation in ancient India.

Recent evidence shows that agriculture was first mastered in Greater India – in the present day Thailand and the Mekong region – no later than 10,000 BCE or 12,000 years ago. Thus, we could surmise that it took about 2000 years for agriculture to make its way from its place of origin to the Sarasvati heartland. This means that the skills needed for growing food grains were already in place in the people, and it was a simple matter to adapt them to the cultivation of newer crops, like wheat and barley, which came to be cultivated later.

VEDIC LITERATURE AND ARCHAEOLOGY

In making the transition from natural history to human history, we are aided immensely by the preservation of a vast body of literature from ancient India. These include the Vedas, the Purans and the epics – Mahabharat and Ramayan. They can be correlated with data from natural history, geology, archaeology and astronomy. The Vedic portrayal of the Sarasvati River, a great river located between the Ganga and the Indus – as the greatest river in India – correlates with geological data and helps confirm the antiquity of Vedic literature. The Vedic goddess of speech has reclaimed her voice and given a new stamp of authenticity on Vedic literature. While one can argue the meaning of words, one cannot as easily argue the course of rivers.

Just as historians could not ignore the role of the ancient literature of the Near East in their archaeological work, they cannot do so relative to India either, whose preserved literature is far more extensive. Archaeology and literature provide the primary material for the reconstruction of any history. As Ancient India is particularly rich in literature, it must be given an even greater place in its case. Putting together the natural history, Vedic literature and archaeology, we can reconstruct a good model of what likely occurred.

However, not only India's ancient literature but even its archaeology is seldom given its due in textbooks today. All of the Near Eastern civilizations of the third millennium BCE, from Egypt to Sumeria, could easily fit within the boundaries of the contemporary Indian civilization centred on the Sarasvati River, which also had cities and writings and the other markers found in the Near East. Because the sites in India were found later by archaeologists, in fact, not until the twentieth century, and were from a culture outside of the traditional boundaries of Western civilization, they were always treated as secondary, though in size and numbers they were greater.

The result has been that India's vast ancient literature and its comparably extensive archaeology have been downplayed and made subordinate to linguistic and ethnological theories that emphasize the importance of the Near East. Yet there has been no proof that India ever borrowed the main aspects of civilization, like agriculture, writing or urban planning from these regions. The speculations that India borrowed its populations or languages have been disproved. Since both were flourishing indigenously India did not have a need for either.

THE LIMITATIONS OF ARCHAEOLOGY

Archaeology provides much useful information, particularly relative to the historical period of the last five thousand years. But it must be adjusted relative to the longer natural history to make sense of the full development of human culture. And it must take into account ancient literature.

We must recognize that archaeology does not provide a complete record of what our ancestors left behind, but of only what little we have been able to recover through our current technological methods of the small portion that has managed to survive the ravages of time. Archaeological remains are haphazard and their interpretation is often highly speculative. Of the extensive archaeological sites found in India, less than one percent have actually been well excavated. It is therefore a serious contraction of any civilization to regard its archaeological remains as a true reflection of its achievements, much less our interpretation of these as a real indication of how this civilization viewed itself.

In addition, archaeology is predominantly land based, and overly dependent on favourable conditions for preservation. It is for this reason that archaeological activity has been dominated by excavations in desert areas like Egypt, Mesopotamia and the Indus Valley. In India this has led to a skewed interpretation, and a neglect of eastern and southern regions, which are much more favourable for human activity. But, because of their moist and rainy climate, and use of wood as a primary building material, they are unsuitable for the preservation of ruins.

Another limitation of archaeology is its ineffectiveness in identifying the remains of maritime nations. Regions that played a key role in the rise of ancient India now lie under the oceans off the coast. While marine archaeology has given us some tantalizing glimpses of what might have been there, these once great landmasses lie permanently beyond the reach of archaeology. As these formed the best habitable lands during the Ice Age and the primary areas of human activity, and as early agriculture has been found in nearby regions of Greater India, it is likely that the basis of other aspects of human culture are also there, but may be well under water and we may never be able to find them.

Early Archaeology: The Gulf of Khambhat

One of the most important finds of recent marine archaeology is the existence of an ancient city in what is now an underwater region in the Gulf of Khambhat

Figure 6: Gulf of Khambhat (Cambay)

(Cambay) which dates to around 7500 BCE (9500 BP). The shelf the site is on went under the sea about 9000 years ago along with the geological changes at the end of the last Ice Age. Recent findings suggest the following.

This city would have been located in the greater Sarasvati river delta of the time. It may reflect the southern roots of the Vedic culture that we are proposing. In Vedic thought, Cambay was in the region of the Bhrigus, one of the greatest ancient Vedic rishi families, and the gurus of Manu. They are related to the nearby city of Bharuch or Bhrigu-kachchh. The Bhrigus were descendants of Varun, the deity of the sea, and were well known for their maritime connections. They were connected to the planet Venus and were great astronomers and architects.

VEDIC AND PURANIC LITERATURE: NATURAL HISTORY AND HISTORY

We need to make a similar transition in our approach to the ancient literature – from accounts relating to natural events like floods and droughts to accounts relating to human activities like wars and the founding of dynasties. We find that the literature does not always make a clear distinction between these two types of events: texts like the Vedas and the Purans treat both as part of the same cosmic phenomenon. However, we can begin by correlating major events in natural history to accounts in the ancient literature. This reveals both the literature and the natural history in a new light.

There are two main sources of ancient literature in India: the Vedas and Purans. The Vedas were compiled at a much earlier era but the Purans contain more historically specific material and sometimes more definite information about earlier eras. Both Vedic and Puranic literature allude to a time when maritime life was important and also describe, in symbolic form, the events that led to post-glacial flooding and the resulting landward migration.

INDRA AND THE ICE AGE

Many scholars have read references to the end of the Ice Age in the Vedic literature, especially in the Indra-Vritra legend that speaks of the deity, Indra, killing the demon, Vritra (the coverer), who holds back the waters, releasing a great flood. Indra is a deity of thunder, lightning and rain, while Vritra is a serpent who holds the waters at the foot of the mountains, suggesting the image of glaciers. Indra destroys Vritra and releases the seven rivers to flow into the ocean, in the process regenerating life on Earth. This Indra-Vritra story is the most persistent legend in the Rig Veda, mentioned in hundreds of hymns such as the following:

> Indra slew the dragon lying at the foot of the mountain. The creator fashioned for him his flashing thunderbolt. As milch cows bellowing as they flowed, directly the waters entered the ocean.
>
> - RV I.32.2
>
> Indra, you destroyed the dragon that withheld the waters. Earth in her awareness furthered your thunderbolt. You gave energy to the ocean-going floods.
>
> - RV IV.16.7
>
> You slew the serpent that encompassed the floods. You released the waters to the ocean.
>
> - RV VI.30.4
>
> Indra, you destroyed the dragon and Heaven approved. You sent forth the flood of the rivers and filled manifold seas.
>
> - RV VI.72.2

Yet, as the Indra-Vritra battle is described as long and difficult, with Vritra rising again several times, it is possible that the story refers not just to the final ending of the Ice Age but to the late Ice Age period with its warm and cool phases before its termination.

PURANS AND THE FLOOD

The Purans contain names and events of many ancient kingdoms and rulers and much interesting information about floods and the dispersal of people from coastal regions. They also contain references to figures before the flood.

All the Purans agree that kings like Vena and Prithu preceded Manu Vaivasvat, the Manu of the flood, in the era of an earlier Manu Chakshusha. This makes them pre-flood or antediluvian kings. Prithu is specifically credited with the creation of agriculture and gave the earth its name, Prithvi. Several other descendants are mentioned in the line of Prithu. Agriculture did begin in this period of a few thousand years before the Ice Age ended lending credibility to this account.

Antediluvian kings and dynasties are mentioned in many other ancient records, including Jewish, Egyptian, Sumerian, Greek, Chinese and Native American. That some sort of culture existed before the end of the Ice Age and was dispersed and passed on at the time of this great cataclysm seems likely. But mainland India was closer to the homeland of pre-Ice Age cultures which flourished further in India and may have better preserved the culture that existed there.

THE TEN AVATARS AND THE END OF THE ICE AGE

Hindu thought recognizes a sequence of divine manifestations or avatars of

Vishnu. While defined primarily in the Purans, some like Matsya, Kurma and Varah occur in the Vedic literature also, starting with the Yajur Veda.

The early avatars – *matsya* (fish), *kurma* (tortoise) and *varah* (boar) – reflect a clear maritime symbolizm. Matsya, the fish avatar, is the same fish that saves Manu and takes him to the Himalayas to preserve the seeds of culture for the coming new age of humanity. The Kurma or tortoise avatar also emerges from the great waters and carries the world.

More specifically, the Varah or boar is the incarnation of Vishnu which saves the Earth and raises it up out of the waters. The unicorn boar or Ekashringa Varah is one of the most common seals from ancient Indian urban sites like Harappa and Mohenjodaro. *That this image dominates the archaeology suggests a continuity of culture going back to the great flood.*

Even the Vaman or dwarf avatar, which describes the ousting of the great maritime world ruler (*Chakravarti*) Bali by a youthful sage, can be read as representing transition from maritime to landward expansion guided by the rishis possessed of special knowledge. While the avatars saved the people and their precious heritage from destruction, they form a part of the teachings that the sages carried with them when population moved to the interior.

Underwater Discoveries

Recent discoveries in marine archaeology help push back the dates of urban settlements in coastal regions, placing them thousands of years before the oldest Harappan cities. Divers of the National Institute of Ocean Technology (NIOT) have found signs of a vast urban site at the bottom of the sea in the gulf of Khambhat

(Cambay). Sonar mapping of the site reveals it to be some 10 km by 2 km in extent, or the size of Manhattan.

Fortunately, man-made objects, including one of wood, have been recovered allowing us to date it. Radiocarbon testing dated the wooden object to around 7500 BCE (9500 BP). Glenn Milne of the University of Durham, using inundation maps and sea level curves estimates that the city may have been submerged 10,000 or even 12,000 years ago. Considering that it is vast and sophisticated, a long period of development must have preceded it. This means the urban culture to which it belonged must be much older.

There are less extensive but tantalizing underwater discoveries off the east coast of India also, near Mahamallapuram and Poompahar in Tamil Nadu. Here too, underwater man-made structures have been found though they have not yet been scientifically dated. The tsunami in these regions in December 2004 revealed the existence of ancient underwater structures that were quite unsuspected. They seem to lend support to ancient Tamil legends that speak of great cities that were submerged by the onrushing ocean floods.

A good deal more marine exploration needs to be carried out, but what has been discovered so far raises the hope that some day, natural history, marine archaeology and oceanic legends may converge and shed more light on our origins with the ending of the Ice Age.

The Vedic Sarasvati Culture

The Sarasvati River is the link between natural history and the Vedic Age. It is the defining data that proves the Vedic nature of ancient Indian civilization. Once we accept the identity of the Vedic Sarasvati and the Sarasvati River of geology and archaeology – which are located in the same place and represent the cradle of civilization for both the literature and the archaeology – all other historical information easily falls into place.

The ecology of the Sarasvati River is central to understanding the development of civilization in North India from 7000 BCE (9000 BP) to the end of the Harappan era around 1900 BCE (3900 BP). Thanks both to science and the Vedic literature, we know a great deal about the Sarasvati River and the civilization it nourished. During its long life, the Sarasvati River went through several changes in its course, gained as well as lost river tributaries, until, in the centuries around 2000 BCE (4000 BP), it became a shadow of itself and eventually ceased as a perennial stream. The chronology of the Sarasvati River is the foundation for understanding the Vedic Age, which was the Sarasvati Age in India.

VEDIC PEOPLE OF THE FLOOD

Rising global temperatures that ended the last Ice Age unleashed two forces of nature that changed the world. First, melting glaciers in the Himalayas released massive quantities of waters that had accumulated in the form of ice and snow over tens of thousands of years. Second, higher temperatures also meant greater evaporation from the seas resulting in much more vigorous monsoons in tropical Asia.

Rivers now became perennial with two sources of water – melting glaciers and abundant seasonal rainfall. Great rivers now watered the once arid North India – the Indus, Ravi, Sutlej, Sarasvati, Yamuna, Ganga and the Saryu. In due course they gave rise to what was to become what many regard as the greatest spiritual civilization in history and also the most enduring. This was the Vedic civilization that flourished in the Sarasvati heartland for over five thousand years.

The summer monsoon rains have always sustained the peninsular rivers from the Narmada in Central India to the Kaveri in the south. In the post-Ice Age period, as the monsoons became more vigorous, the flow in the peninsular rivers became greater. Human settlements, which during the Ice Age subsisted by precariously hugging the scarce freshwater sources that dotted the coastline and the hillsides, found they could now expand inwards.

While peninsular India with its long coastland remained a major area of human activity, the greatest attraction was the northern plain transformed by the great Himalayan rivers. It also provided a safe haven from the rising waters along the coasts. Long adept at maritime activity, people from coastal regions of tropical Greater India moved into the now fertile lands in the Indian heartland.[27] They carried the agricultural skills that had evolved in Greater India and adapted them to the Sarasvati-Indus plains and delta. The vast plain of North India provided them better arable land than the coasts of Greater India and a cultural and agricultural revolution and expansion occurred.

The man who led the people to higher ground, taking them all the way to the upper reaches of the Sarasvati River and the Himalayan foothills, is called Manu in the Vedic literature. Yet Manu referred not just to a person but also to a culture, a way of life and a spiritual system, the teachings of Dharma. Manu had with him great sages, the legendary seven rishis, who were a repository of spiritual and yogic knowledge. He took with him the essence of the older southern culture and planted its seeds along the fertile northern rivers.

This means that both those who claim that the Vedic culture is indigenous to India and those which hold there was an older pre-Vedic, more correctly proto-Vedic culture, in the south, are right. Vedic culture in North India developed from the older southern culture carried on by Manu. But it grew up in North India as the Ice Age ended. The Sarasvati River was its matrix, a river that was not substantial during the Ice Age and which after 2000 BCE (4000 BP), again lost its prominence.

MANU AND HIS PEOPLE

Manu is not only a Vedic flood figure, but also part of South Asian mythology extending into Indonesia. He is mentioned in several ancient works including the Rig Veda, where he is the dominant background teacher. The Vedic teaching is essentially the teaching of Manu as carried down and expanded by various rishis. Manu himself was a rishi or a fount of wisdom. He was also a great yogi according to the Bhagvad Gita. He was also the original king and lawgiver for ancient India. Similar Manus are mentioned in other Indo-European traditions and similar ancient progenitors occur in all ancient traditions, many of which are flood figures. Even the Rig Veda mentions different Manus as Vivasvan, Savarna and Samvarana.

The Shatapath Brahmana (SB I.8.1) first contains the Manu flood in detail.[28] During his morning ablutions in the water, Manu found a small fish in his hands.

The fish warns him that a massive, all consuming flood will come in a certain year and instructs Manu to build a ship. It begged him to save its life and promised in return to save him and his people from the impending calamity. Manu cared for the fish that gradually grows in size. He transferred the fish from a pot, to a pit, and eventually to the sea. Then when the flood came the fish told Manu to tie the rope of his ship to his horn and the fish takes Manu to the northern or Himalayan mountains for safety. The mountain where the fish took Manu was called Manoravasarpanam or Manu's descent (SB I.8.1.6).

Descending from their refuge in the Himalayas, Manu led his people to the banks of the Sarasvati beneath the Himalayan foothills and established a great dynasty that produced both kings and sages who created and sustained the Vedic civilization. Manu's fish became the fish or Matsya Avatar of Lord Vishnu. In the Matsya Puran, Manu did his austerities on the Malaya Mountains in Kerala, showing his southern origins.

We may say that Manu observed signs of a major flood that threatened him and his people. He led his people to higher ground and eventually settled them in the Sarasvati heartland. [29]

Manu had a daughter called Ila, who symbolizes his teachings. Ila is another name for Sarasvati, along with Bharati as the third. Ila is said in the Rig Veda to be one of the first teachers of humanity. From her the lunar dynasty (Chandra Vamsha) of Vedic kings arose. Yet Ila also has a masculine form, emphasized in the Purans. From him the solar dynasty (Surya Vamsha) of Vedic kings arose. This story of Manu's daughter, Ila, turning into a man may be read as a change from matriarchal to patriarchal practice. Tradition places Manu in what is now Kerala where royal succession has always been through the female line. Manu himself is a solar figure and son of the Sun deity, Vivasvan.

SARASVATI AND THE VEDIC CIVILIZATION

Sarasvati, unique among Vedic rivers, is a great goddess, the subject of three entire hymns[30] and mentioned over sixty times in the Rig Veda. No other river has such a status. The Rig Veda provides the same importance to the Sarasvati that was later given to the Ganga in the post-Vedic age. In one verse (VII.94.8),[31] Sarasvati is described as "singular among the rivers, pure in its course from the mountains to the sea." It is described as a large ocean-going stream.

The Sarasvati was not only the holiest river, but also the greatest. She is the best of the seven rivers and the Mother of the rivers, the Mother of Sindhu.[32] She overflows with the rivers or Sindhus (RV VI.52.6).[33] Sarasvati is the best of the seven rivers (RV VI.61.9-10). It is fed by three, five or seven streams (RV VI.61.12) and nourishes all the five Vedic peoples. According to Bharadvaj of the sixth book (VI.61.2), the Sarasvati, in flowing through the mountains, "crushed boulders like stems of lotus plants."

Great Vedic rishis like Vasishtha and Jamadagni (RV VII.96.3), Gritsamada (RV II.41.16) and Bharadvaj (RV VI.61) are connected to the Sarasvati, as also are great kings like Divodas (RV VI.61) and Bharatas like Devavat and Devashravas (RV III.23). It is particularly important for the Purus, the main people of the Rig Veda ("Sarasvati, on both whose plant-laden banks the Purus dwell." RV VII.96.2). There is a special prayer to never leave her banks, "Sarasvati, may we not leave you for other lands."[34]

From all this we learn that the Sarasvati was the most important river for the Vedic people spiritually and culturally, their central land and place of origins, and that it also sustained large populations. This idea finds expression in this verse by Gritsamada (VI.41.16): *ambitame, naditame, devitame Sarasvati,* "Sarasvati, the best of mothers, the best river, the best goddess." The Vedic civilization was therefore the 'Sarasvati civilization'. That is how the Vedic poets described it and is also what archaeologists and geologists are finding.

The location of the Sarasvati River in India is clear from the famous *Nadi Sukta* of the Rig Veda (X.75.5), which places the Sarasvati between the Yamuna and the Shutudri (Sutlej). Enumerating the rivers from east to west, it says:

imam me gange yamune sarasvati shutudri stomam parushnyā;

asiknyā marudvridhe vitastyā arjikiye shrinuhyā sushomayā

Ganga, Yamuna, Sarasvati, Shutudri (Sutlej), Parushni (Ravi)

Asikni, Manuvridha, Vitasta, Arjikiye, Shrinuhya and Sushomaya

Since the *Nadi Sukta* mentions rivers eastwards from the Ganga to the Indus, locating the Sarasvati in Afghanistan as some modern scholars want to do would require us to shift the Ganga, Yamuna and several other rivers also to Afghanistan. More importantly, the verse helps us locate the Sarasvati – firmly between the Yamuna and the Sutlej, the place of the great post-Ice Age river, which can hardly be a coincidence.

SARASVATI – RIVER LOST AND FOUND

Today there is no major river flowing between the Yamuna and the Sutlej and there has not been one for several thousand years. This led some scholars to dismiss the Vedic Sarasvati as the imagination of poets or to place it in Afghanistan, identifying it with the small Haraqiti in Afghanistan because Haraqiti is cognate etymologically with Sarasvati. While this idea was invented to explain the importance of the Sarasvati River in the Vedas before the time the Sarasvati River was discovered by modern geology, it has persisted even beyond that point.

According to this view, the memory of a small Afghani river was brought to India by the invading Aryans is what is found in the Rig Veda. However, this view has two major problems. Afghanistan is a landlocked country, and the Haraqiti does not flow "from the mountains to the sea" and is not a major river at all. This is not easy, considering that not only the Rig Veda but also later literature like the Brahmanas and even the Mahabharat describe the Sarasvati River and its surrounding landscape in detail. It is more likely that Vedic people moving into Afghanistan named a river there after their greater and more glorious Sarasvati in India. Besides, the Vedic literature shows a contact with the river at all its phases from its arising as a mighty stream at the end of the Ice Age to its termination as a major river around 1900 BCE (3900 BP).

From the later Vedic literature starting with some Brahmanas like the *Panchvimsha* and the Mahabharat we learn that the Sarasvati was no longer the mighty river described in the Rig Veda, though there is a memory of its previous greater glory, and had actually split into two parts, one drying up in the desert of Rajasthan and the other starting further down and still reaching the sea as a small stream. In other words, the great ocean-going Sarasvati of the end of the Ice Age is clearly described in the Rig Veda, while the phases of its drying up occur in later Vedic and post-Vedic texts. The Vedic people not only were acquainted with the river but with its entire natural history. This would not be possible if they contacted the river only at the late stages of it's drying up or if their original Sarasvati was located elsewhere.

Some scientists, however, took the Vedic accounts seriously. Investigations were not long in coming. As far back as 1886, R.J. Oldham of the Geological Survey of India concluded that a great river with its course lying between the Yamuna and the Sutlej did exist in ancient times as described in the Rig Veda. He located its upper course along the seasonal stream Ghaggar in Haryana. He noted that there were significant differences between the Sarasvati of the Rig Veda and the Sarasvati described in the later literature, suggesting that the Vedic Sarasvati was this larger, older, long dried up stream. Oldham based his conclusions on the similarity of fossil remains along the course of the dry riverbed.

Oldham's work, though quite thorough, was ignored by historians who remained attached to the idea that the Vedic Aryans came to India in 1500 BCE (3500 BP) and composed the Rig Veda only in 1200 BCE (3200 BP). To them, Sarasvati was only a deity worshipped in the form of the river. When archaeologists unearthed the Harappan civilization (or Indus civilization) in the early twentieth century, they failed to note its link to Oldham's Sarasvati River. Though initial archaeologists like Wheeler knew of Oldham's work, they ignored or dismissed it. It was only after 1950, when it is was clearly established that most of the Harappan sites were on the dried banks of the river that Oldham had identified as the Sarasvati, and that the drying up of the river had ended the Harappan age, that opinions began to be revised.

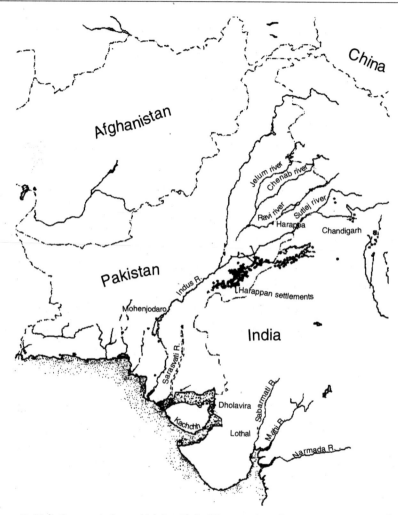

Figure 7: Vedic Sarasvati along which late Vedic (Harappan) settlements were concentrated

It soon became clear that a large number of Harappan settlements lie not on the Indus, but at locations from 40 to 120 kilometres to the east of it. Hundreds of sites have been found in Cholistan in the Bahawalpur district of Pakistan. Today, there is no major water source in the region, but there must have been a great river when these sites were flourishing or they could not have existed. The same situation is encountered in parts of Rajasthan and Kachchh, where ancient settlements occur in areas where there is little water today. All this indicates that a major river must have been flowing through the region in ancient times. You can't have such settlements where there is no water.[35] The natural explanation is that what sustained this civilization was the Sarasvati described in the ancient literature, which the texts locate in the same regions.

Beginning in 1978, another form of direct evidence became available through satellite images acquired by earth sensing satellites launched by NASA (National Aeronautics and Space Administration) and ISRO (Indian Space Research Organization). These showed traces of ancient river courses (called palaeo-channels) that lay along the course of the Sarasvati River described in the ancient literature. *They show a channel ranging in width from 6 to 8 kilometres, exceeding 14 kilometres in places, which is larger than the Ganga today.* This established the existence of the Sarasvati beyond all doubt as a great river.

Recent geological studies have traced different stages of the flow and drying up of this great river. Broadly speaking, there were two main phases of Sarasvati – the wide ocean-going Sarasvati and the declining Sarasvati, a weakened river that over time no longer reached the sea but dried up in a series of lakes in Rajasthan.

VEDIC AND LATE-VEDIC SARASVATI

Here is the picture we get when we look at some recent findings in geology, satellite photography and water sampling. The great Sarasvati River described in the Rig Veda as flowing from the "mountains to the sea" is very ancient. The latest data places this phase primarily between 8000 and 5000 BCE (10,000 and 7000 BP), in the main post-Ice Age warm period during which there was the greatest glacial melt, though the river had already begun to flow during the warm periods before the Ice Age ended a few thousand years before this period. This is in agreement with what we know of the natural history of the Himalayas following the Ice Age. In its upper reaches, the Sarasvati flowed through the Ghaggar channel, now represented by a seasonal stream.

What made the Rig Vedic Sarasvati a mighty river was the flow it received from two glacier-fed Himalayan rivers, the Yamuna and the Sutlej, as well as the great glacial melt from the region as a whole. Over time the Yamuna changed its course and began to flow east into the Ganga. This reduced the flow into the Sarasvati, leading to a weakening of its upper course. Then the Sutlej turned away from the Sarasvati to the south west, cutting off its main perennial source of water (the Sutlej arises in the trans-Himalayan region). The glacial melt similarly declined over time.

The result was that the Sarasvati no longer reached the sea and disappeared into the desert at a place called Vinashana, where a series of lakes formed instead. This place of its disappearance is located in Rajasthan and Haryana, where it retreated over time. Scientists have also found signs of at least one earthquake that could have caused the river to change course, which occurred around 3000 BCE (5000 BP). This situation of the Sarasvati no longer reaching the sea corresponds to the description found in the later Vedic literature, including some Brahmanas and, most notably, the Mahabharat. The Mahabharat speaks of this region of lakes as Samanta-panchaka, created at the time of Parshuram.

The specific dates have not yet been firmly determined by science, but it is clear that by 3000 BCE (5000 BP), the Sarasvati was already in decline and by 1900 BCE (3900 BP) it had ceased to exist as a major perennial stream. In other words, *the Harappan civilization existed during the late Sarasvati period or along the declining Sarasvati River, while the older portion of the Vedic age was long before this, when Sarasvati was still the greatest river in the region.* The termination of the Sarasvati River corresponds with the end of the Harappan Age. It was the drying up of the Sarasvati that caused the Harappan decline and the abandonment of its cities. To date, not a single Harappan site has been found to have been destroyed by outside invaders.

This means that the main reason for the fall or end of Harappan culture (or the Indus Valley civilization as it is sometimes called) was ecological changes and not any invasion – Aryan or otherwise, as many had thought. Besides losing the waters of the Yamuna and Sutlej, there was a worldwide drought in the 2200 to 1900 BCE (4200 to 3900 BP) period that struck across a wide belt from southern Europe to China. It ended the civilizations of Egypt in the Old Kingdom and Sumer-Akkad in Mesopotamia along with the Harappan.[36]

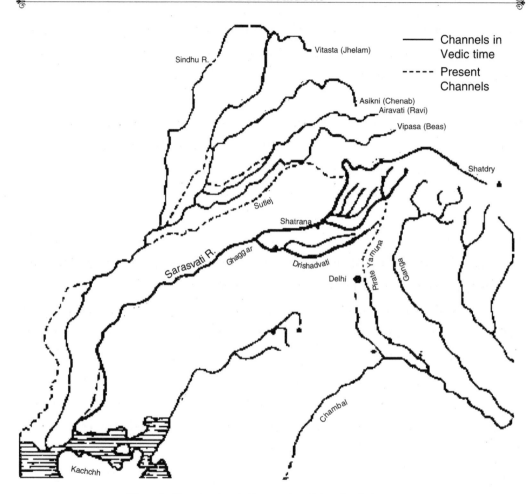

Figure 8: Map showing the Sarasvati and the related rivers systems.

We may summarize the situation as follows: the Sarasvati described in the Rig Veda flowed through what is now the Ghaggar channel, a seasonal stream in Haryana. It had two major tributaries – the Sutlej and the Yamuna. The Yamuna, or a major effluent of it, flowed into the Sarasvati via the Chautang channel. The Chautang too is a seasonal stream today. This, along with the glacial flows, made the Sarasvati a mighty river like the Ganga. By 3000 BCE (5000 BP) it began to decline and by 1900 BCE (3900 BP) it came to an end as a great river, with the Sutlej breaking up and shifting away.

After that the Sarasvati became a minor season stream flowing through the Ghaggar channel. It remained only as a memory and a place visited by devotees, as it is today. Even the Mahabharat, though it speaks of the Sarasvati drying up in the desert, remembers numerous sacred sites along it associated with great Vedic rishis like Vasishtha and Vishvamitra, and kings like Bharat and Kuru, the same figures that dominate the older Vedic literature.

The Sarasvati River, the main goddess, voice and homeland of the Vedic culture, has loudly proclaimed its existence through geological studies, thus verifying the antiquity of Vedic cultures that Western historians, with their obsession with the West as the origin of all civilization, had so far failed to understand. This should put an end to all speculation relating to the Aryan invasion as the cause of the collapse of the Harappan Civilization. What ended the Vedic Age was not any invasion but the drying up of the Sarasvati.

THE GREATER VEDIC LAND: THE LAND OF ILA AND KURUKSHETRA

It is not just the Sarasvati, however, that was the land of the Vedic people and their related groups, but the entire region of North India from the mountains to the sea.

The Sarasvati-Drishadvati region is the central holy land of the Vedic people and of Manu, also called the 'place of Ila'. This land, which is located in the Rig Veda between the Sarasvati and Drishadvati rivers (RV III.23.4), is a great place of kings in the Rig Veda. It is also the holy land of the Brahmins, from which the great Vedic teachings originate (MS II.17) according to Manu Smriti.

> O Agni, we place you down on the best place on Earth, in the place of Ila, in the brightness of the days. At the place of Manusha on the Drishadvati, Apaya and Sarasvati Rivers, shine forth resplendent.
>
> - RV III.23.4

Agni (also called Ila in the masculine sense), like a father, is first enkindled at the place of Ila by Manu (RV II.10.1). This is the central place of the great Vedic rituals. In the feminine tense, Ila Varta is identified specifically as the Sarasvati-Drishadvati region later called Khandava and Kurukshetra and is a very sacred area. This is said to be the best place on Earth, which is also the place of Sudas and the Bharatas (RV III.53.11), great Vedic kings. It is called the centre of the Earth (RV III.29.4; X.1.6). Such sanctity reflects the antiquity and importance of the Sarasvati river in the post-Ice Age glacial melt.

THE LAND OF THE SEVEN RIVERS

The Vedas are not limited to the Sarasvati alone but describe a land of many rivers flowing to the sea. The number of rivers is specifically said to be seven, a figure that occurs many times throughout the entire text.[37] The main term for river is Sindhu, so the land of the seven rivers is Sapta Sindhav. The ancient Persian scripture, Zend Avesta (Vendidad Fargard I.20), similarly knows of a land of seven rivers (Hapta Hindav). These rivers can be identified with the seven goddesses, identified as mothers, streams or voices that give birth to Agni, the fire deity (RV III.1.4), or the seven Mothers of Soma (RV IX.102.4). They are the mothers of Indra (RV VIII.96.1), the greatest of the Vedic deities, to whom all hymns flow like rivers to the sea (RV I.11.1). The rivers are sacred to all the main Vedic deities, whose worship extends to all of them.[38]

The Atharva Veda speaks of seven rivers that extend over a region like heaven and earth (AV IV.5.2). Modern scholars have generally identified these with the rivers of the Punjab (five river region of northwest India) with Sindhu and Sarasvati. However, in Vedic literature, the Sarasvati, located in the easternmost section of the Punjab, is the most important of the seven rivers (RV VI.52.6). *Therefore, the land of the seven rivers cannot be limited to the Punjab,* nor can the seven rivers be all made into tributaries of the Indus, nor can Sarasvati be made their easternmost. The land of the seven rivers must have included rivers to the east of the Sarasvati and outside the Punjab. This is confirmed as eastern rivers like Yamuna, Ganga (also called Jahnavi) and Saryu are also mentioned in the Vedas as big rivers.[39] Such a land of many mighty rivers could hardly be located in arid Afghanistan or Central Asia.

THE IMAGE OF THE OCEAN: CONTINUED MARITIME CONNECTIONS

The Vedic culture was the result of a maritime culture that moved northward into the Sarasvati plain. Yet it maintained its connection to the sea, particularly through the Sarasvati delta region in the Rann of Kachchh. The background image of the ocean dominates the Vedic mind.

The Rig Veda, the oldest Vedic texts, contains more than 150 references to the ocean, including the mention of rivers flowing into the sea and travel by sea. Whole theories of the location of the Vedic people have been built around a few scanty references to rivers like the Kubha in Afghanistan, while much more common references to the ocean are ignored. Only one river, the Sarasvati, has an extensive mythology about it. Yet the ocean not only has an extensive mythology about it, there is much oceanic symbolizm about all the main Vedic deities, including Indra, Agni, Soma, Surya and Varun, to name just a few.[40]

References occur to two oceans, eastern and western (RV X.136.5), to inferior and superior oceans (RV VII.6.7; X.98.6), or to two seas called *samudra* and *purisha* (RV I.163.1; IV.21.3). There are additional references to four oceans, corresponding to the four directions.[41] These four oceans may relate to the eastern, western and southern seas, and to the lake in Kashmir in the north. An ocean with seven foundations is described (RV VIII.40.5). Sometimes the Rig Veda speaks of many oceans.[42] Given India's proximity to the Arabian Sea, Bay of Bengal and the Persian Gulf, this idea of several oceans is not surprising. The common Vedic anointing of kings in the Brahmanas (AB viii. 15) is "from one end up to the further side of the earth bounded by the ocean as sole ruler."[43]

The seer Vasishtha, the greatest of the Vedic seers, is himself a descendant of

Varun, the deity of the sea, and achieves his enlightenment while travelling on the sea.

> When Varun and I ascend into the ship, when we go forth to the middle of the sea, then we move with the waves of the waters and swing back and forth as if on a swing for joy. Varun placed Vasishtha in a ship. Skillful, he made him into a seer by his greatness. A sage, he made him a singer in the brightness of the days, as far as the heavens extended, as far as the dawns.

> - RV VII.88.34

Vedic cosmology also views the universe as a series of oceans and creation as an overflowing of a primeval sea.

> Law and truth from the power of meditation were enkindled. Thence the night was born and then the flooding ocean. From the flooding ocean the year was born. The Lord of all that moves ordained the days and nights. The Creator formed the Sun and Moon according to previous worlds; Heaven and Earth, the atmosphere and the realm of light.

> - RV X.190

It is said of the Eskimos, that because of their great familiarity with snow, they have many words for it in their language. Similarly, Vedic Sanskrit also has numerous words for the sea often indicating finer nuances. Among the commonly used words are: *samudra, salil, sagar* and *sindhu*. The word *sindhu* can mean either the sea or a large river, and sometimes even the river Indus. It is interesting that one of the words for a mariner is *sindhuka*, deriving also from the root *sidh*. And *sindhuka*, Sanskrit for sailor, became Sindbad the Sailor when stories from India found their way into the famous *Arabian Nights*.

Western India was then dominated by the delta of two great rivers – the Sarasvati and the Sindhu (Indus). These stretched from the west of the Rann of Kachchh almost to Bhrigu-kachchh or the modern Bharuch. People of the Indus delta were known as Saindhavas, which can also mean maritime people, deriving from the same root *sidh*. This vast coastal region into which flowed navigable rivers was ideal for the development of maritime civilization.

All this indicates that Vedic society (of which Harappan was a part) was a complex mosaic in which riparian and ocean navigation played a major part. This helps explain the presence of many maritime and riparian stories in works like the Mahabharat. Bhishma is said to be the son of Ganga – a river goddess. This can mean that Ganga belonged to a river tribe that was part of a maritime society. The same is true of Satyavati, whose father was the chief of a fishing tribe. The word *apsara* (*ap-sara*), which is often taken to mean a celestial nymph or a mermaid, literally means 'she who moves in the waters'. Quite obviously this can refer to a woman from a maritime tribe.

Vedic seers like Vasishtha and Agatsya were said to be sons of *apsaras*, or women from maritime tribes, like Urvashi. That their father was Varun, the ocean, simply means that he belonged to an ocean-going tribe, just as Ved Vyas was known as Dvaipayan or 'Son of the island' because he was born on an island. Vasishtha and Agatsya were known as Maitra-Varuni or 'Son of Mitra and Varun' meaning simply that they were sons of a tribe connected to the sea deity Varun and his companion Mitra. Again the Bhrigus were descendants of Varun, also referring to their hailing from coastal regions.

No ancient Indian work – beginning with the Rig Veda, the Purans, and the epics – describes a nomadic people or society. They are the products of a settled civilization with a very large maritime component. Of all the statements made about the Vedic people and the Vedas, none is as baffling as the claim that the Rig Veda does not know the ocean. Nothing could be further from the truth. This should serve as a sobering pointer to the great deficiency of scholarship making such claims. When they have so grossly misinterpreted the Vedas by describing a maritime people as steppe nomads, what trust can we place in their other opinions?

VEDIC PEOPLE: YADUS AND PURUS

The two most important people of the Rig Veda are the Purus (later known as Kurus) and the Yadus. The Sarasvati flowing from the Kurukshetra of the Purus in the north to the southwest coast where the Yadus lived would have connected these two ancient and important people.[44] Since the great delta of the Sarasvati provided an outlet to the ocean, the maritime nature of Vedic society becomes easy to explain. This also explains the concentration of Vedic seers in two places – the Bhrigus in the southwest by the sea, and the Vasishthas and Angirasas in the Kuru heartland in the north, with much overlap between the two.

Since Vedic society was maritime in nature with more and larger rivers flourishing in North India at the time, it may not be easy to find and explore archaeological remains from that period which may now be under water. Yet some archaeological evidence is now lending support to the idea that Vedic India had a strong maritime component. At an international conference on seafaring held in 1994 in Delhi, several papers were presented showing that Indian cotton was exported to South and Central America going back to 2500 BCE (4500 BP) and even earlier. One author presented evidence for the possible presence of Indian cotton in Mexico as far back as 4000 BCE (6000 BP). According to Sean Mcgrail, a marine archaeologist at Oxford University, seagoing ships called 'clinkers' that were thought to be of Viking origin were known in India a good deal earlier. A PTI story filed on 7 March 1994 reported:

> Cotton from India reached Latin America at least 4000 years before Columbus, carried across the oceans by ancient mariners who had mastered long-distance navigation. That fascinating theory emerged at an international scientific meeting. Scholars from six countries also said that *ancient Indian boat-building and navigational skills have remained unrecognized.* (Emphasis added.)
>
> "India was one of the earliest sites where maritime contacts flourished," said Jean-Francois Salles, a French archaeologist. "The bulk of the exchange between the 4500 year old Indus civilization and West Asia was by sea." The discovery that a hybrid variety of cotton was growing in America long before Columbus reached there in 1492 CE has triggered speculation that cotton from Asia, specifically India, was carried there well before 2500 BCE (4500 BP).
>
> The northwest part of the Indian subcontinent had by 2500 BCE (4500 BP) established a very strong tradition of cotton. This makes India one of the most likely sites of origin of the cotton taken to the Americas. ...
>
> "Seafarers from this country [India] used constellations, the position of the pole star, and the movements of the sun to chart out nautical routes," said B. Arunachalam, ...
>
> The hybrid variety of cotton called 'tetraploid' cotton was growing in Mexico as early as 4000 years BCE (6000 BP) and fabrics based on this cotton dating back to 2500 BCE (4500 BP) have been found at a site called Husca Preita in Peru.

This means that Indian cotton could have reached Mexico before 4000 BCE (6000 BP), taking us to the Rig Vedic Age. It also explains why such a sophisticated harbour like Lothal, an important Harappan site excavated by S.R. Rao, was in operation by 2500 BCE (4500 BP) in India: it was needed to support this maritime trade.

HARAPPANS OF THE SARSAVATI – LOST OR MISUNDERSTOOD CIVILIZATION?

What country had the largest urban civilization in the early ancient period from 3100 to 1900 BCE (5100 to 3900 BP)? One might expect that it was Sumeria or Egypt. *Perhaps surprisingly to many, the correct answer is India, through the Indus or Harappan civilization.* Ancient India possessed an urban civilization that covered a larger area than both Egypt and Mesopotamia put together, which were the main contemporary urban civilizations of the time.[45] It was more sophisticated and standardized in terms of town planning, roads, sewage and draining, and patterns of communication over distant regions.

Such an early urban civilization must have had a profound impact on the culture of India for many centuries, establishing its foundations and creating its unique characteristics for all of history. It is here that we are likely to see the basis of India's arts, crafts, building skills, agriculture, and its intellectual and spiritual culture. It must have had a profound impact on the other surrounding civilizations of the times, particularly smaller Sumeria and Babylonia, with which it had extensive trade contacts.

One of the great mysteries, if not deficiencies, of ancient history as it is viewed today is that so little emphasis is given to the ancient urban culture of India relative even to the civilization of India, much less relative to that of surrounding regions. Regardless of its size and sophistication, the Harappan civilization is generally treated as a sidelight to smaller Western cultures.

It is our view here that the culture, populations and languages of this urban civilization of ancient India have endured and are reflected in the dominant culture, populations and languages of the region down to the present day. The characterization of this culture as a 'lost' or 'forgotten civilization' reflects more a modern inability to understand it.

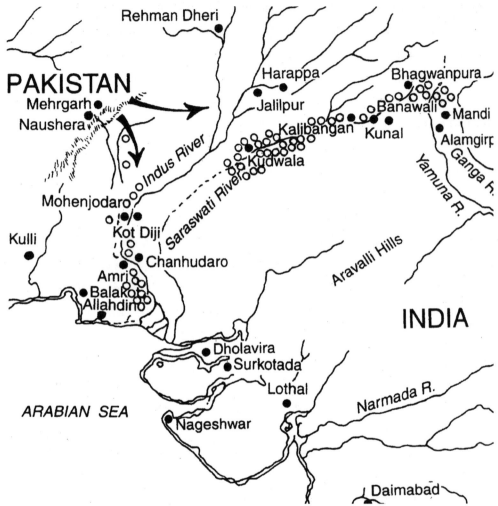

Figure 9: Map of the Sarasvati showing the major Harappan sites. Note the concentration of sites near the Sarasvati. (The National Museum, New Delhi)

HARAPPAN, INDUS OR THE LATE SARASVATI CULTURE

The term Harappan civilization refers to the vast complex of settlements unearthed by archaeologists beginning about 1921 and continuing to the present. The first site to be excavated was Harappa on the Ravi River in the Punjab, soon followed by Mohenjodaro in Sind, both now in Pakistan. The leading archaeologists were Daya Ram Sahni, Rakhal Das Bannerji, and Sir John Marshall, then Director General of the Archaeological Survey of India. These two sites are only two of the more than 2000 settlements – numbers keep growing with new finds – found on both sides of the border.

Today, more than two thirds of Harappan sites can be found on the Sarasvati River banks or in its delta region by the Arabian Sea. This includes several sites like Rakhigarhi and Ganweriwala that are larger than Harappa and Mohenjodaro. Rakhigarhi, the largest of these sites, is located in the Kurukshetra region east of Delhi, the old homeland region of the Vedic kings. Other important sites include coastal centres like Lothal and Dholavira in the coastal delta of the Sarasvati River, showing the strong maritime activity of the Harappan people. While most textbooks still highlight the sites of Harappa and Mohenjodaro from decades ago as if they were the last word, many new discoveries continue and even more sites have not yet been excavated. If anything, the Harappan civilization was probably larger and older than what we have found so far.

Harappan sites can be found over a vast area in excess of 1.5 million square kilometres. They extend from the Amu Darya River in Afghanistan to the Ganga in the north and from the border of present day Iran to close to Mumbai in the South. Harappan sites were built over a very large span of time, dominating the period from

3100 to 1900 BCE (5100 to 3900 BP) and are connected to pre-Harappan and post-Harappan sites as well.

Initially, the Harappan was called the 'Indus civilization', but the term has fallen out of use, now that it is known that the Indus was not its central region. Other scholars have proposed renaming it the 'Sarasvati civilization' or 'Indus-Sarasvati civilization'. Yet no matter what name we use to call it, it is important to recognize that the settlements are clustered around the Sarasvati River and it ended when that river went dry around 1900 BCE (3900 BP). After that the people shifted but the same culture continued in surrounding regions of India. It didn't come to an end but only went through what archaeologists like James Schaffer of Case Western University in the USA call a relocation phase (1900-1300 BCE, 3900-3300 BP), after which the classical civilization of ancient India developed.

Ever since the Harappan civilization came to light, the main question has been: what is the relationship between Harappan archaeology and the Vedic literature? The more we look at the totality of data, the conclusion becomes clear. *Harappan archaeology represents the material remains of the culture and civilization described in the Vedic literature, particularly during its later period.*

THE PEOPLE OF INDIA AND THE CULTURE OF INDIA

We cannot separate the development of culture and civilization in India from its people. We cannot attribute the dominant civilization of the region to outside influences of small groups of people coming in from the northwest during the late ancient period (after 1500 BCE, 3500 BP), such as European theorists first proposed in the nineteenth century. The culture of India was already developed by that time and had been urbanized for about fifteen hundred years before it. Just as the human types remained, the culture would have also survived.

Skeletal remains from ancient India, such as those from Harappan sites four thousand years ago, show the same basic ethnic types as in modern India. These include groups just like North Indians, Dravidians and Munda people who inhabit the region today. It means that the same types of people that we see in India today were responsible for the culture and civilization of the region in ancient times.

The peoples of India have always had the numbers to maintain and preserve their own culture. This does not mean that there was no borrowing from outside of India or even migrations into India that had their impact in many ways. There were, similarly, movements of people and cultures out of India. However, we do not need to ascribe the origins of the type of civilization that has developed in India and is unique to India to outside people, migrations or borrowings from cultures in different geographical regions. Just as the peoples of India have maintained themselves genetically, so too, their culture has continued and grown. With much more clearly defined geographical boundaries than Europe or Mesopotamia, India had a much more self-contained environment for cultural growth.

The Ancient World's Largest Literature and Largest Urban Culture

India is unique among all ancient civilizations in that it has preserved largely intact its ancient literature. This is because India maintained the continuity of its civilization and ancient religion, while other ancient cultures, even those as great as Egypt and Greece, could not survive the onslaught of time.

This Vedic literature from ancient India is the largest that has survived from anywhere in the ancient world. The four Vedas and their commentaries number well into the thousands of pages and were finalized long before the time of the Buddha some 2500 years ago. By some accounts, including those in this book, the Vedas are 5000 years old or more.

Composed in a complex set of metres, Vedic texts cover an entire range of spiritual, religious and social topics, showing an old culture that had its own unique view of life. However, by the views of modern historians, who have been inclined to look for the basis of Vedic literature outside of India to the northwest, there is no civilization or archaeological remains that can be associated with this Vedic literature. *We are left with the mystery of the most extensive literature of the ancient world without any settled civilization to create or sustain it, eventually adapted by an entire subcontinent that it was originally alien to and whose indigenous literature it cruelly replaced and removed all traces of!*

Similarly, the Harappan ruins represent the largest urban culture in the ancient world at its time (3100-1900 BCE, 5100-3900 BP), as we have already noted. However, so far no literature has been attributed to this vast Harappan culture, even though it was literate and has left us many writing seals. *We are left with the mystery of the most extensive urban civilization of the ancient world not leaving any literary record for itself or having any identifiable impact on the literature that came later, even though it was a literate culture that managed to produce thousands of beautifully inscribed seals!*

In short, we are left with the mystery of a literature without a civilization and a civilization without a literature. This is particularly odd because the Vedic is traditionally the literature of ancient India, of which the Harappan is the archaeological remains. So, if we put these two factors together, connecting the civilization and literature of ancient India, we solve one of the great problems of ancient history.

Since the literature and archaeological ruins both reflect the same geographical area of the Sarasvati River in North India, it is easy to equate them, if we but set aside the preconceptions that would separate them. This means that we should use Vedic literature to understand Harappan ruins and vice versa. The Sarasvati River provides the link. Yet Vedic literature reflects not only aspects of the urban phase of ancient India but its antecedents going back to the Ice Age, so we must look at it according to that broader time frame as well.

FLORA, FAUNA AND CLIMATE IN THE VEDAS

The main flora and fauna of the Vedic texts, back to the Rig Veda, is that of India.[46] The flora in the Rig Veda includes such typical Indian species as lotuses (*pushkar, padma*), bamboo (*vaamsha*), *durva, shara* and *munja* grasses, *khadir, kimsuka* and *shalmali* trees. The Vedic sacred fire or Agni is enkindled with the wood of two sacred trees, the *ashvattha* and the *shalmali*, both native India species and both mentioned in the Rig Veda. The *ashvattha* known as *Ficus religiosa* is the most sacred of the Rig Vedic trees as it is that of the Upanishads and later India. It is still sacred.

The fauna of the Rig Veda is yet more obviously Indian including peacocks (*mayur*), swans (*hamsa*), water buffaloes (*mahish*), *gaura* (another type of buffalo or the Indian bison), the humped back or Brahma bulls (*vrishabh*), lions (*simha*), boars (*varah*), camels (*ushtra*) and elephants (*hasti*) – all of which are common to the region. The Atharva Veda, which mentions more species, features the whole array of India's plants and herbs and other animals. Harappan seals contain images of these same plants and animals. *The species of plants and animals depicted on Harappan seals are the same as those found in the Vedic literature.*

The climate mentioned in the Rig Veda reflects a great monsoon, with rain deities like Indra and the Maruts taking prominent roles in the Rig Vedic hymns. The Vedic geography is of a land of many rivers, many mountain ranges, deserts, wide forests and the sea, much like India today. Agni, the Vedic fire deity, is often specifically a deity of the forests.

We don't find any significance given to a cold climate or Central Asian plants and animals, which would be the base if the Vedic people had come from that region. The Rig Veda has nothing in common with the proposed Proto-Indo-European homeland of birch forests and steppes of Central Asia. There are no statements in the Rig Veda, like those in the Bible, of a group of people coming in from a far off region. There is, on the contrary, an immemorial regard for the motherland of great rivers, the Sarasvati homeland.

HARAPPA AS THE LATE VEDIC AGE

The Vedic and Harappan were not separate civilizations, but only earlier and later phases of the same civilization, with some degree of overlap. Otherwise, we are left with a host of contradictions and paradoxes that no amount of ingenuity can resolve. The most glaring one of these is that if the Vedic people (Aryans) arrived in India in 1500 BCE (3500 BP) and composed the Rig Veda in 1200 BCE (3200 BP), they would have filled the book with praise for the Sarasvati River that had dried up 500 years before they arrived and whose scope that they lauded had ended even many centuries before that!

Harappan archaeology represents the closing phase of the Vedic civilization that began when the Sarasvati was flowing from the 'mountains to the sea'. It ended when the

Sarasvati dried up completely between 2200 and 1900 BCE (4200 and 3900 BP). The Harappan period was the late Vedic Age. This means that there is a greater urban component and other cultural developments in Harappan that reflect more the later Vedic texts, like the use of bricks which is a common theme in the Yajur Veda. To understand the Vedic-Harappan connection we must look to the entire Vedic literature, not just the Rig Veda.

HARAPPAN SEALS: LANGUAGE AND WRITING

The Harappans were a literate people, leaving behind more than three thousand seals and other artifacts, many of them with short inscriptions. There is a great deal of uniformity of the types of seals found from different sites, just as the urban planning of the Harappan cities follows similar patterns, though covering a vast geographical region.

Harappan seal writing goes back 5000 years, making it contemporary with the oldest writing of Sumeria. The writing mainly consists of a few letters on small seals. Large inscriptions have yet to be found, rending the decipherment yet more difficult. However, along with the writing there are many symbols, constituting the main form of iconography from the culture. These include many Vedic symbols as we will discuss in the upcoming iconography section.

The writing has remained unread for nearly a century, partly due to the notion that the Harappans were non-Vedic and therefore the language of the seals could not be Sanskrit. Some scholars pointed out that the Harappan script, though complex, bore many similarities to the later Brahmi script used all over India and Greater India for writing Sanskrit, but they were largely ignored.

Using these two as clues, the eminent Vedic scholar and paleographer Natwar Jha claims a fundamental breakthrough that has enabled him to read a large number of seal inscriptions.[47] Jha's proposed decipherment shows that the language of Harappan inscriptions is Vedic Sanskrit. It is later than the language of the Rig Veda, similar to the Sanskrit used in the later Vedic literature like the Upanishads. This is exactly what one would expect, considering that the Upanishads, like the Harappans, came after the Rig Veda.[48]

However, this is a technical issue and the decipherment is still controversial. We only note that Jha's decipherment and the readings fit naturally into the historical and chronological scheme we follow in this book. *Whether one accepts this particular decipherment or not, the Vedic nature of the Harappan symbolizm and their continuity with later Hindu images and practices is quite clear.*

Some examples of the decipherment given by Jha and Rajaram in their book follow. Note that the examples and readings, as well as the iconography follow the Vedic symbolizm discussed later in the chapter.

inah suretah

dhāvatyātmā

shānta (or *shānti*)

trāāe indrāāvah   *deva rāpa*   *agni saha*

Figure 10: Examples of deciphered seals (Jha and Rajaram, The Deciphered Indus Script)

There is a good deal of other evidence, not only from India, but also West Asia showing that Harappans belonged to the later Vedic period and their language is early, meaning pre-classical Sanskrit. These range from Vedic mathematical texts (the famous *Shulba Sutras*) to trade records between the Harappans and the Sumerians – their contemporaries in Mesopotamia.

Ancient Symbols

VEDIC SYMBOLIZM IN HARAPPAN ARCHAEOLOGY

A picture can speak a thousand words and communicate directly to us what no amount of writing or logic can convey. In the following figures, simply look at these images of Harappa and see what they convey to you of their own accord. The images of Harappa are clearly early images of India's characteristic spiritual civilization, following the same basic symbols, practices and motivations as found in later India of the classical period. The continuity of culture is undeniable, which requires a continuity of people and teachings as well.

Once we recognize that the Harappans were the people of the Vedic Age, the meaning of the images contained in Harappan seals and other artifacts becomes clear. This is a vast subject, so we will limit ourselves to just a few examples. The connections go very deep.[49]

SWASTIKA

Figure 11: Svasti symbols and message: panca-svasti-adma (or vidma) refers to the panca-svasti mantra.

We begin with a fairly straightforward interpretation, the sacred *svasti* symbol or swastika. (Swastika stands for *svasti-ka,* meaning 'maker of welfare'.) The swastika is a common Hindu, Buddhist and Jain emblem of good fortune and was generally regarded by Western archaeologists as a sign of Aryan settlements. It indicates the wheel of the Sun and the wheel of Dharma. It is also common in ancient Harappan sites in India and is one of the most common symbols of India's perennial civilization.

Swastikas appear singly as well as in combination with other signs in Harappan sites. The photo above shows a string of five *svasti* signs.[50] It can be related to the sacred *svasti mantra* found in the Yajur Veda (25.18 –19), reflecting yet older Rig Vedic verses, in which the word 'svasti' (welfare) appears five times. The ancient Taittiriya Aranyaka uses it for its opening passage. It may be paraphrased as:

We invoke Him who may bring us welfare.

May the respected Indra guard our welfare,

May the omniscient Pushan guard our welfare,

May the Universal Creator guard our welfare,

May the Great Protector bring us welfare.

The Harappan swastika images are obviously related to such Vedic prayers, which are still used today to sanctify homes and mandirs.

THE VARAH AVATAR

The most common Harappan symbol is a one-horned animal that most take as representing a boar. It occurs on hundreds of seals, far more than any other pictorial symbol. Again there is a clear Vedic equivalent. The Varah or boar incarnation of Vishnu is well known. In the Mahabharat, it is also described as one-horned *(eka-shringa)*.

Figure 12: The so-called 'unicorn' bull, but actually the varah

Ekasringah pura bhutva varah divyadarsanah

Imam codddhrtavan bhumim ekasringastato hyaham

In ancient times I assured the form of the one-horned boar as a divine apparition,

To lift the earth out of the waters. Hence I was called one-horned.

- Mahabharat, Mokshadharma Parva 330.2751

This seal is particularly important for showing how the Harappan age reflects the late Vedic age when the Varah avatar was more common. While the Varah is mentioned a few times in the Rig Veda, the idea of it as an avatar occurs first in the Yajur Veda.

All this universe in the beginning existed as the fluid of the waters. In that the Lord of Creation (Prajapati), moved, becoming the wind (Vayu). He saw this world, becoming a boar (Varah), he grasped it, becoming Vishvakarma (the form fashioner), he shaped it. This world extended and became the Earth (the wide one). That is the Earth nature (prithivtvam) of the Earth (Prithvi).

- Taittiriya Samhita VII.5.1

The boar incarnation of Vishnu lifts the Earth out of the waters, which can also be taken as the waters of the flood at the end of the last Ice Age. This Yagna-

Varah or sacrificial boar is one of the dominant markers of Harappan culture and spirituality.

This one-horned boar often appears something like a bull. In this regard the Rig Veda also speaks of the *vrisha* Varah, the male or bull boars that accompany the deity Brahmanaspati (RV X.67.8), who like the Harappan Varah are associated with the cauldron (*gharma*), used for sacrificial offerings.

THE PASHUPATI SEAL

Figure 13: The famous Pashupati seal

This famous seal shows a three-headed deity seated in a Yoga posture as the god of wild animals. Many have identified it with Bhagwan Shiv as Pashupati. It is probably the most famous of all the Harappan seals and has inspired more discussion than any other. The Rig Veda also describes deities like Agni as three-headed ("We laud Agni who has three heads and seven rays," RV I.146.1). Agni is also called Rudra in the Rig Veda. The rulership over the animals is ascribed to various Vedic deities, Agni, Indra and Rudra-Shiv. The Pashupati is seated in an advanced yogic posture (*asana*) known as *mula-bandha-asana.*

The seal contains a meditating horned deity along with five animals. The five animals are – elephant, musk deer, buffalo, tiger and rhinoceros. These five animals can be identified with the five senses and the five associated elements – fire, water, space, wind and earth. These elements that make up the material universe are known in the Vedic literature as *panch maha-bhuts* or the Five Great Elements.[52]

VEDIC SHIV LINGAS

The Shiv Linga is an integral part of the Hindu religion. It is reflected in Harappan artifacts as well. This further identifies the Harappan era with the late Vedic era during which Shiv became predominant as we see in texts like the Yajur Veda (the Rudram) and the Atharva Veda (the Vratya). Some scholars have tried to divide off the worship of Shiv from the Vedic religion. They forget that in the Rudram, the most famous Vedic chant and most famous chant to Shiv, Shiv is honoured as the personification of the Vedic offering or Yagna. As Rudra, Shiv is identified with Agni, the Vedic fire deity.

FIGURES IN YOGA POSTURES

Figure 14: Harappan figurines in different yogic postures (asanas)

There are several seals as well as terra cotta figurines demonstrating various *asanas* or yogic postures. Here is one set of examples. This shows that the Harappans had knowledge of Yoga practices, including *asanas,* that most scholars would date thousands of years later.[53] It indicates the continuity of India's mystical traditions from the earliest times. Such seals also prove the yogic meaning of other Harappan symbols, like the Pashupati symbol.

THE SEVEN GODDESSES OF THE PLEIADES

Figure 15: The seal of seven goddesses

The above seal shows seven goddesses and several animals worshipping a single figure coming out of a stylized pot or base of an *ashvattha* tree.

This seal has an important astronomical meaning. The seven goddesses are the seven stars of Krittika or the Pleiades, who are also in Vedic thought the wives of the seven rishis. Their son or child is Agni, the fire deity, whose sacred tree is the Ashvattha tree. As the Rig Veda notes, "The Seven voices conceive Agni as a single child (RV III.1.6)." Even in India today, depictions of the seven goddesses and their son is common.

Krittika as marking the vernal equinox is a common theme in later Vedic texts and lists of the *nakshatras* (constellations or the lunar mansions). It would have occurred astronomically in the period from around 2800-1800 BCE (4800-3800 BP) or the Harappan Age, as we will discuss in more detail relative to Vedic astronomy. Seven is a sacred Vedic number relative to goddesses, rishis, forms of the Sun deity (Adityas), rivers and other factors. Many such Harappan deities have horns as do many Vedic deities.

THE WATER BUFFALO

After the unicorn boar and the humped bull the water buffalo is perhaps the most common Vedic seal. The water buffalo or *mahish* is a common Rig Vedic animal associated primarily with Soma but also with Agni and other deities. Soma is said to be the Mahish among the animals.

> Soma flows as the father of thoughts, the father of Heaven and the father of the Earth, the father of Agni and the father of the Sun, the father of Indra and the father of Vishnu, Brahma among the deities, the one skilled in metres among the poets, the rishi among the sages, the water buffalo (*mahish*) among animals.

> - RV IX.96-5-6

The water buffalo is an important domesticated animal for rice, sugarcane and water agriculture, which is connected to Soma as the deity of water and fertility.

THE BRAHMA BULL OR BULL OF DHARMA

The typical humped back or Indian Brahma bull occurs on numerous seals. Its identification with dharma is well known. In Vedic thought, the bull, *vrishabh,* is most closely connected to Indra, the foremost of the Vedic deities, and is perhaps the most common animal that he is identified with (note RV II.16.5-6, for example). It is also a symbol of the Purush, as the cow is of Prakriti. Brihaspati or Brahmanaspati, the Vedic deity of prayer and dharma, is also commonly called a bull or *vrishabh*. As the prototype for the later deity, Brahma, perhaps the Brahma bull was named after him.

> The bull of the peoples, who has all forms and is inviolable, Brihaspati, the most adorable.
>
> - RV III. 62.6

MULTIHEADED ANIMALS

Harappan seals show many imaginary or mystical animals with multiple heads or body parts. Such animals are also common in Vedic literature. The Rig Veda III.56.3 notes, "The bull with three flanks, all forms, three udders, creating progeny in many places, he has three heads and rules as the great one; he is the seed-giver, the bull of the eternal ones." Such multiheaded deities later became typical of Hindu iconography.

VEDIC FIRE ALTARS

The Vedic religion was characterized by the worship of fire as *Agni*. The Harappan culture also was based on fire worship with fire altars commonly found at Harappan sites. Most interesting is a group of seven fire altars found at Kalibangan. Kalibangan is located at the confluence of the Sarasvati and Drishadvati Rivers, the central point of Brahma Varta, the ancient Vedic sacred land as mentioned in texts like Manu Smriti. It was the main focus of the region of Kurukshetra that the two rivers define. This place where the rivers met was famous for its sessions of the Vedic rishis. The seven fire altars at Kalibangan confirm this ancient tradition.

Figure 16: A row of seven fire-altars at Kalibangan

WATER TANKS

Along with a ritualistic worship of fire, the Vedic tradition had a similar worship of water and ritualistic bathing. This is reflected in the great water tanks that are found in Hindu mandirs even today. Such great water tanks are well in evidence at Harappan sites, like the great bath at Mohenjodaro.

Figure 17: The famous 'Great Bath' at Mohenjodaro

THE SPOKE WHEEL SYMBOL

A six-spoke wheel is a common Harappan symbol. It suggests knowledge of spoked wheels and their usage in chariots, which the Vedic people appear to have first invented. Yet it is also an astronomical symbol of the wheel of the Sun and the six seasons of the Hindu year.

OM SYMBOL

Another important Vedic symbol appearing on Harappan artifacts is what we interpret as the OM sign. The figure below displays line drawings of the seal in two positions – original and rotated by 90 degrees. The one on the right – i.e. rotated by 90 degrees – resembles the Devanagari OM. Scripts like Kannada and Telugu reflect more the orientation of this Harappan OM, while elongating it a little. All of them can be traced to the Harappan OM. The photo and the line drawings display

Figure 18: The OM on a seal (omkar mudra). The second line drawing shows how the devanagari OM is derived from the Harappan OM. Note the sacred ashvattha leaves on the OM seal.

only the most ornate OM signs found; the same shape appears on scores of Harappan artifacts.

This 'bow-shaped' Harappan OM carries profound Vedic symbolizm. The Mundaka Upanishad (2.2.4) states, "Pranav (Om) is the bow, the soul is the arrow, and Brahman is the target. With full concentration, aim at the target and strike, to become one with Brahman, just as the arrow becomes one with the target." This is almost a visual description of OM as found on a Harappan seal.

The OM, which is adorned by *ashvattha* leaves and branches, highlights the sacredness attributed to the *ashvattha,* a Vedic idea. The Katha Upanishad (2.3.1) describes the *ashvattha* (pipal) tree as embodying the essence of sacredness, "This is the eternal *ashvattha* tree, with the root at the top but the branches downwards. It is He that is called the Shining One and Immortal. All the worlds are established in Him, none transcend Him." The same idea is echoed in the Bhagvad Gita (15.1): "That *ashvattha* tree with its root above and branches down, whose leaves are the Vedas, is imperishable. And he who knows this knows the Vedas."

The *ashvattha* is the seat of sacred knowledge and the abode of the deities. This idea goes back to the Rig Veda itself (X.97.5), its famous Hymn to the Plants: "Your abode is the *ashvattha* tree; your dwelling is made of its leaves."

* * *

These images represent but a small sample of the deep Vedic symbolizm that pervades Harappan archaeology. In summary, the Vedic and Harappan civilizations were one, with Harappan representing mainly the later phase of the Vedic culture. Harappan artifacts are material representations of ideas and thoughts found in the Vedic literature extending to the Upanishads. All this data has been around for eighty years. We are astonished that even such obvious Vedic symbols like the swastika signs, fire altars and the OM should have been missed by scholars. This can only be due to an attachment to a fixed idea and a refusal to see the evidence in front of one's own eyes.

The conclusion is obvious: Harappans were the Vedic Harappans.

ARCHAEOLOGICAL CONTROVERSIES: THE ELUSIVE HORSE

There are various reasons why Western scholars, and some Indian as well, resist the idea of a Vedic basis to ancient India's civilization. Most of them have not studied Vedic culture from primary sources. Many are influenced by nineteenth century views that had little regard for non-European cultures. Many have not examined the new evidence from archaeology, geology and natural history.

The curious thing is that such scholars ignore the broad mass of evidence which equates the two, whether the rivers systems and geography of the Vedas, the similar ancient fire religion, or the many similar customs and artifacts. They emphasize what they say is not there, looking for an exception to focus on to prove their case. It is like saying that a man who has described an animal with tusks, a snout and long ears cannot be referring to an elephant because he has not mentioned that it has four legs.

It seems that such scholars have an ideological or cultural resistance to equating Vedic culture with that of Harappan India. Indeed, it would require a complete rewriting of ancient history, if not a new view of who we are as a species, if India rather than Greece or Palestine was our true cultural homeland, and if yogic spirituality rather than scientific materializm or religious monotheism was the highest goal of civilization! One wonders if their bias in favour of the Western idea of civilization has not clouded their vision on these issues!

Of course, one must realize first that the Vedic literary record, which is a specific compilation at a certain point in time, and a randomly discovered archaeological record, cannot totally reflect one another. It is enough if the main points correspond. Here we will briefly examine the most contended points. The reader should also look back to our Vedic-Harappan gallery for the more obvious correlations.

THE HORSE EVIDENCE

Some scholars have objected to the Vedic-Harappan connection because of what they regard as the lack of horse remains or horse depictions in Harappan sites, as compared to the frequent Vedic references to horses.

First, a study of horse anatomy shows that there were two types of horses in the ancient world that we still find today. There is an Indian type that has seventeen ribs and a West and Central Asian horse that has eighteen ribs.[54] The Rig Vedic horse, as described in the Ashvamedha or horse-offering of the Rig Veda, has thirty-four ribs (seventeen times two for the right and left side).[55] This shows that the Rig Vedic horse did not come from Central Asia but was the South Asian breed. The Rig Vedic horse is born of the ocean, which also indicates southern connections.[56] The Yajur Veda ends with an invocation of the divine horse that has the ocean as its belly — *samudra udaram* (TS VII.5.25).

Meanwhile, most Harappan seals depict mythical creatures like a unicorn boar, including a number of multi-headed creatures, and so cannot simply be looked at as a zoological index of all the animals used at the time. Even the Vedic horse is described as limbs of a deer and wings of an eagle (RV.I.163.1), golden horns and copper feet (R.I.163.9), hardly a representation of a biological horse.

Relative to the idea some people have that there are no horse remains at Harappa, horse bones have been found at all levels at several Harappan sites. Sir John Marshall who excavated Harappa and Mohenjodaro gave measurements of the horse remains he had found at Mohenjodaro (see his *Mohenjodaro Indus Civilization,* Vol. II, pages 653-4). Clay horse figurines, like the terracotta horse, have also been found from Lothal. In this regard, noted archaeologist B.B. Lal states:

Even the much-touted argument about the absence of the horse from the Harappan Civilization has no validity in the light of the new evidence regarding its presence. The noted international authority on the palaeontology of the horse, Sandor Bokonyi of the Archaeological Institute, Budapest, after duly examining the faunal remains concerned, had declared as far back as 1993 that 'the domestic nature of Surkotada horse (a Harappan site in Kachchh) is undoubtful.'[57]

Harappan civilization extended to Afghanistan (Bactria), a region famous for its horses, so we would expect horses at Harappan sites and as some part of Harappan culture in any case. Yet most importantly, *we do not find any evidence of a horse culture coming into India around 1500 BCE (3500 BP)* in the form of horse remains, horse encampments or horse images. These Aryan horses have never been found anymore than the Aryan people have! If the Aryans came with the horse around 1500 BCE (3500 BP), such remains would have to be dramatic. If the horse were indigenous to India, on the other hand, there would not be dramatic horse remains at one level as opposed to another. So far there are no significant horse finds at any level of Indian history, even later when horses were well known.

Even in the Bactria and Margian Archaeological Complex (BMAC), which is supposed to be horse rich and a staging area of successive Indo-Aryan migrations/invasions into India, not a single horse bone has been found. This means that other areas supposedly rich in horses do not exhibit significant horse remains either.

In addition in Vedic literature, it is not only the Vedic people but also their enemies who are portrayed as having horses. "They gained all the wealth of the Panis, replete with horses (*ashvavantam*), cattle (*gomantam*), beasts and men (RV I.83.4)." The Vedic literature does not show a battle between a group with horses and those without but with two groups who had the same basic culture, artifacts and weapons.

Moreover, there are many equus bones found in ancient India, particularly the onager (*Equus hemionus*), which is native to Kachchh in Gujarat. There is evidence that the onager was used to draw chariots or battle cars in ancient Sumeria and was later replaced by the stronger and faster horse. The same thing probably occurred in India. It is also likely that the Vedic people did not discriminate between the different equus animals as strictly as we do, and did not radically mark off the true horse from other related breeds. This means that the Rig Vedic horse (*ashva*) could have, at least in the beginning, been an onager, which explains its oceanic connections as its native region of Kachchh is along the sea in what would have been the delta of the Sarasvati River.[58]

Other scholars have noted that the Rig Veda knows of a light, spoked-wheel chariot that did not appear in the Middle East until around 2000 BCE (4000 BP), suggesting that the text must be later than this period. They point out the lack of chariot remains in Harappan sites. Countering this view, the spoked-wheel is a common Harappan writing symbol, which we noted in the previous iconography section. So, there is evidence that the spoked wheel chariot had considerable antiquity in Harappan India. Curiously the old horse training manuals in the Hittite language around 1400 BCE (3400 BP) reflect Sanskrit terms, which can also be interpreted that horse culture came from India.

In addition, the dominant animal is the Vedic bull, often described as humped, like the humped Brahma bull, which we do find on Harappan seals. The Indian bull is an indigenous animal and the same is true for the Indian cow, the Vedic sacred animal per se. Horses were important animals of the aristocracy, but have never been numerous in India at any period. Their Vedic depictions reflect their usage in fighting, not necessarily the fact that horses were found everywhere the same way cows were. The Rig Veda was very much a book of the nobility or Kshatriya and so may have given more emphasis to the horse image for that reason as well.

Chronology

We include the different aspects of chronology as a single section for easy access by the reader. The details behind these chronologies as well as references to them can be found in other chapters of the book. These chronologies will cover the period from the late Ice Age to the end of the Vedic or Sarasvati civilization in India. We can divide this into two eras: Pre-Sarasvati River era and Sarasvati River era. These are generally the same as the Pre-Vedic or Proto-Vedic and the Vedic.

The late Ice Age period, roughly from 15,000 to about 10,000 BCE (17,000 to 12,000 BP), was the time in which the climate and the environment underwent cataclysmic changes, radically altering the basis of human culture and leading to the world as we know it. It saw the agricultural revolution begin, and expand into mainland India, leading to the Sarasvati civilization. Though there have been great climate changes in the past ten thousand years, they have been nothing like what went on during this period. This information is available in scholarly books and scientific journals and is mainly the subject of natural history.

For the Sarasvati period from 8000 to 3000 BCE (10,000 to 5,000 BP), which we regard as the main Rig Vedic Age, our sources are works on natural history supplemented by the publications of the Geological Survey of India, and, more recently, satellite studies by the Indian Space Research Organization (ISRO), which detail the course and changes in the Sarasvati and related rivers. This scientific data has been supplemented by our readings of ancient Indian texts – the Vedas, the Purans and the epics – the Ramayan and the Mahabharat. We have been particularly sensitive to references to natural changes and maritime activity, which lie at the heart of the early Vedic and Puranic cultures and their earliest rishis, kings and kingdoms. Archaeology begins to come into play here as well.

When we come to the later Sarasvati period, or the Harappan period (3000-1900 BCE, 5000-3900 BP), we have the voluminous post Rig Veda literature to rely on – a corpus that includes the Yajur, Atharva and Sama Vedas, the early *Sutra* literature, the Upanishads and the Brahmanas, and of course the epics, notably the Mahabharat. This contains often detailed information on the course of rivers and astronomy that helps us further in the dating of events. In addition, we have massive archaeological evidence from the many Harappan urban sites.

Beginning about 3000 BCE (5000 BP), we get inscriptional data, not only from the Harappan sites, but also from Mesopotamia, which had maintained trade and diplomatic relations with Harappan India. These, however, are supplementary and go only to confirm and support the information obtained from the main sources.

CHRONOLOGY 1: PRE-SARASVATI TO SARASVATI ERA

Ancient Indian chronology, to some extent still followed in textbooks, was formulated at a time when natural history was little understood, Indian archaeology was virtually nonexistent and Vedic texts were denigrated by colonial scholarship. This resulted in a highly compressed chronology that sought to fit the whole of the Vedic civilization within a few centuries beginning in 1500 BCE (3500 BP) as largely a borrowing from the outside.

Since our study takes us back to the Ice Age, we have found it necessary to enlarge the scope and meaning of the word chronology.[59] We approach chronology from two perspectives – natural and historical. Natural chronology refers to assigning dates to natural events like the ending of the Ice Age, submersion of coastal lands, the rise of the Himalayan rivers and the drying up of the Sarasvati River. Cultural counterparts can only be general for us, with regard to early periods.

DATE	NATURAL EVENT	PLAUSIBLE LITERARY ACCOUNT
17,000 BCE (19,000 BP)	Late Ice Age	Coastal cultures in Greater India, the idea of pre-flood civilizations
15,000 BCE (17,000 BP)	Warming begins; unstable coastline	Coastal cultures under stress
13,000 BCE (15,000 BP)	Ice Age ending; flooding begins of coastal regions. North India gradually opens up for habitation	Proto-Vedic civilization mainly in the south of India
11,000 BCE (13,000 BP)	Younger Dryas (glaciation); freeze returns	Indra-Vritra battles
10,000 BCE (12,000 BP)	Farming spreads in Greater India and the Indian interior	Indra-Vritra battles
8000 BCE (10,00 BP)	Renewed warming. Ice sheets finally retreat. Great North Indian rivers (glacier fed) begin to flow. Monsoon stronger. Sarasvati becomes the greatest river and Sarasvati-Drishadvati *doab* becomes the Rig Vedic home	Vritra the coverer slain by the solar deity Indra. Beginning of the Rig Vedic Age in the Sarasvati heartland, Manu of the flood

Table 1: Pre-Sarasvati era (Pre-Vedic and Proto-Vedic)

Table 1 gives what we call the natural chronology of the Pre-Sarasvati period, which is also that of the end of the Ice Age.

CHRONOLOGY 2: THE VEDIC SARASVATI ERA

The main conclusion to follow from nearly a century of research in archaeology, natural sciences, palaeography and literary studies may be summarized in a single statement: *The Vedic Age is the Sarasvati Age.* While the details may still be developing the overall picture is clear. The development of civilization on the Sarasvati River which archaeology shows is reflected in Vedic texts.

Vedic dynasties would reflect the same time periods. Approximately five thousand years, from about 7000 BCE (9000 BP) to 2000 BCE (4000 BP), saw the rise and fall of great dynasties – the Ikshvakus (Rama's dynasty), the Purus and the Yadus. It saw two great catastrophes – the Mahabharat War and the decline and the ultimate drying up of the life-giving Sarasvati River.

DATES	NATURAL/HISTORICAL EVENT	HISTORICAL DEVELOPMENTS
10000 BCE (12,000 BP)	Sarasvati region begins to open up in the late Ice Age Period	Indra-Vritra Battles
8000 BCE (10,000 BP)	Beginnings of the post-Sarasvati settlement	Manu Vivasvan period
7000-4000 BCE (9000-6000 BP)	Prime era of ocean-going Sarasvati	Early Vedic dynasties: Yayati, Turvash, Yadu and Puru. The early rishis: Angirasas, Bhrigus, Bharadvajs, Vamadev
4000-3000 BCE (6000-5000 BP)	Weakening of the Sarasvati; end of early Vedic Age	Great kings of the Ikshvakus and the Puru-Bharats. Trasyadasu, Mandhata, Bharat. Late Vedic rulers, Ram, Sudas and the Pancals. The Battle of Ten Kings. Vasishtha and Vishvamitra
c. 3100 BCE (5100 BP)	Traditional date of Krishna	Compilation of the Vedas under the Purus. Mahabharat War. Ved Vyas and his pupils compile the Vedas
3100-1900 BCE (5100-3900 BP)	Harappan civilization on the declining Sarasvati	Late Vedic and early Puranic Age
2200-1900 BCE (4200-3900 BP)	Worldwide drought – Europe to China Sarasvati dries up	End of the Late Vedic Age. The focus shifts east to the Gangetic plane
1900-1300 BCE (3900-3300 BP)	Post-Harappan relocation period	Some Vedic peoples move out of India to the West

Table 2: Vedic period from the early dynasties to the end of the Sarasvati River

CHRONOLOGY IN HARMONY WITH TRADITIONAL HINDU LITERATURE

In this proposed chronology we will try more specifically to relate Vedic literature with geological events and the different stages of the drying up of the Sarasvati river. So far there is no evidence that would cause us to reject the 3100 BCE (5100 BP) date for Krishna and the Mahabharat War. Recent astronomical evidence (reference) also confirms it.[60]

Harappan civilization was sustained by the later Sarasvati period, when the Sarasvati was declining and would eventually lose both the Yamuna and Sutlej. This alone is sufficient to show that the Harappan civilization had to be later than the Rig Veda.

PERIOD OR DATE	EVENT OR EPISODE
15,000 BCE (17,000 BP)	Glaciers begin to retreat
12,000 BCE (14,000 BP)	Release of the rivers; ocean levels begin to rise
10,000 BCE (12,000 BP)	First agriculture begins with rice domestication in the Mekong region using lake overflows and hill slopes
c. 8000 BCE (10,000 BP)	Agricultural revolution spreads to river deltas in Greater India and to India. The Sarasvati and the North Indian rivers
8000 to 7000 BCE (10000 to 9000 BP)	Inundation of coastal lands and possible exodus to Sarasvati led by Manu. Descendents of Manu's daughter Ila establish ruling dynasties
8000 to 4000 BCE (10,000 to 6000 BP)	Sarasvati at its greatest, flowing from the "mountains to the sea". The age of the Rig Veda
6000 to 4000 BCE (8000 to 6000 BP)	Global climatic optimum – maximum rainfall. Possible founding of the Bharatas
4500 to 4000 BCE (6500 to 6000 BP)	Gradual loss of the Yamuna. Exile of some Bharat kings like Samvarana
4000 to 3500 BCE (6000 to 5500 BP)	Sutlej-Sarasvati becomes the main river. Pressure on the land. King Sudasa repels an attack by a confederacy of ten princes. This is known as the Battle of Ten Kings. Compilation of the Rig Veda

begun by the Vasishtha clan under Sudasa's patronage. Vasishtha-Vishvamitra rivalry. The period of Ram and Ramayan

3500 to 3000 BCE	The return of Samvarana's descendant, Kuru, who begins the Kuru rule
(5500 to 5000 BP)	Period of turmoil
c. 3100 BCE	The Mahabharat War; Krishna's death
(5100 BP)	
c. 3050 BCE	Takshak kills the Kuru King Parikshit (Arjun's grandson)
(5000 BP)	
c. 3000 BCE	Janmajay (Parikshit's son) sacks Takshashila. First recitation of the Mahabharat.
(5000 BP)	
c. 3100 to 1900 BCE	The later Sarasvati or the Harappan civilization. Vedant works
(5100 to 3900 BP)	
c. 2200 to 1900 BCE	Sutlej shifts west and flows into the Indus. A severe drought brings about the decline and dispersion
(4200 to 3900 BP)	of the Harappans
c. 1900 BCE and later	Activity moves to the Ganga and the Gujarat coast. Great kingdoms give way to *janapadas*. Some
(3900 BP and later)	migrating Kshatriyas conquer Mesopotamia and establish the Kassite Empire

Table 3: Broad chronology from the Ice Age to the end of the Sarasvati

ANCIENT KING LISTS AND CALENDARS

Vedic literature has provided extensive lists of kings and much information on ancient calendars that is invaluable both for dating the Vedic period and for understanding its profound spiritual culture. When the Greeks came into contact with India about the time of Alexander (300 BCE, 2300 BP), they found that the Indians had a record of over 150 kings going back 6400 years or to around 6700 BCE (8700 BP):

From Father Liber to Alexander the Great, they reckon the number of their kings to have been 154, and they reckon 6,451 years and three months.

From Dionysus to Sandrocottos, the Indians count 153 kings and more and 6042 years and during this time, thrice for liberty... this for 300 years and the other for 120 years.

6700 BCE (8700 BP) is also notable because it reflects an era 3600 years before the 3102 BCE (5102 BP) date of the Kali Yug and shows the existence of a previous 3600 year cycle. Father Liber is Father Manu. Placing Manu as the first king around 6700 BCE (8700 BP) agrees very well with the time period of the end of the Ice Age. His story as a flood figure coming from the south similarly agrees quite well with the timing and movement of peoples that the ending of the Ice age brought about. That the Hindu king lists and geology correspond is not surprising, given how the Sarasvati River information also corresponds with the events of natural history.

Curiously the Hindu Purans do record 153 kings between Manu and Chandragupta (Sandracottus), but Chandragupta Gupta, not Chandragupta Maurya. But in any case they provide a long record of rulers, many more than Egyptian or Babylonian lists, which could reflect dynasties going back to such an early era. Hindu records and dynasties agree well with what natural history tells us occurred, starting the first kingdoms about the time the Sarasvati area became agrarian. They don't show any migration into India by a group of people in the late historical period but the records of the indigenous culture of the region going back to the end of the Ice Age.

CHRONOLOGY AND ARCHAEO-ASTRONOMY

Another source of chronology is astronomical in nature. It reflects the recently arisen new science of archaeo-astronomy, which dates eras by their astronomical references. As the points of the solstices and equinoxes relative to the fixed stars change over thousands of years, one can identify eras by their marking stars, should there be any record of these. When we remember that ancient people used the sky as their calendar, that they would note the stars marking these important times of the year cannot be ignored.

Vedic texts provide ample evidence for archaeo-astronomical research. *Jyotish* or astronomy was called 'the eye of the Veda'. This is because it was the foundation for the timing of the rituals around which Vedic culture was based, and for the whole calendar according to which planting and harvesting of crops and other important actions were based. The main Vedic ritual, the fire ritual (*gavam ayana*), began with the winter solstice and followed a reverse order after the summer solstice, making the points of the solstices and equinoxes central to their orientation.

The Vedas use a system of 27 or 28 *nakshatras* or lunar constellations in order to divide the heavens and mark the movement of time. The *nakshatras* reflect the most natural and scientific way of looking at the heavens because the moon transits one *nakshatra* every day. Such changes can be easily observed by everyone. This *nakshatra* system is another important Vedic scientific discovery. Even in the Mahabharat, we find a tradition of days named after the *nakshatra* in which the moon was positioned. The equinox or solstice points of *nakshatras* change every thousand years and so help us calculate the eras in which they were placed.

In this regard, we find that Krittika or Pleiades (which mark the early portion of the sign Taurus among the 12 zodiacal constellations) head the list of *nakshatras* and are related to the vernal equinox in most of late Vedic literature. They are so mentioned in many places as in this late hymn of the Atharva Veda:

Easy to invoke, O Agni, may the Krittikas and Rohini be, auspicious Mrigashira and peaceful Ardra. Graceful be Punarvasu, beautiful Pushya, bright Aslesha, with the solstice at

Magha for me. Virtuous be Purva Phalguni and Uttara, Hasta and Chitra peaceful and may Swati give me joy. Bounteous Vishakha, easy to invoke, Anuradha, the best *nakshatra* Jyeshta, I invoke, and Mula. May Purva Ashadha provide me nourishment and Divine Uttara Ashadha give me strength. May Abhijit provide virtue, as Shravana and Shravishta grant beauty. May Shatabhishak give me greatness for expansion, and the two Proshtapadas give protection. May Revati and Ashwayuja give me fortune and Bharani grant me wealth.

- AV XIX.7.24.

Besides starting with the Krittika as the eastern direction and spring solstice, the same hymn uses the term 'ayana', which specifically means solstice in later astronomical literature, which it places in Magha. When the vernal equinox was in the Krittika (Taurus), then the summer solstice would have been in Magha (Leo), thus confirming the statement.

The Shatapath Brahmana similarly states, "The Krittikas do not swerve from the eastern direction, all the other constellations do (SB II.1,2,3)." East is the direction that marks the vernal equinox. The Taittiriya Brahmana states, "One should consecrate the (sacred) fire in the Krittikas (individual stars); the Krittikas are the mouth of the *nakshatras* (TB I.1.2.1)." The Krittika equinox and Magha solstice refers astronomically to a period from around 2500-1800 BCE (4500-3800 BP) or the late Harappan Era. It takes Vedic astronomy back into the Harappan period.

One specific astronomical text has survived in Vedic literature. This is *Vedanga Jyotish*. It is a calendar work and indicates a time in which the summer solstice was in Aslesha and the winter solstice in Shravishta, a date of around 1300 BCE (3300 BP). This information is also mentioned by the great astronomer Varahmihir, "There was a time when the southern course of the Sun began from the middle of Aslesha (23° 20′

Cancer) and the northern from Nishta (Shravishta or Dhanishta), for so it has been stated in ancient texts. These now take place from the first points of Cancer and Capricorn (0° Cancer)." (Brihat Samhita, III.1)

Yet earlier references and mythologies exist in Vedic literature, indicating times in which the vernal equinox was in Rohini (mid-Taurus) or Mrigashira (0° Gemini), taking us back many more centuries yet. While these references are not as clear as those in the Krittikas, they fit in well with the movement of civilization and natural history. The 3102 BCE (5102 BP) calendar of traditional Hindu thought is of the Rohini equinox. The Mahabharat War is associated with a special Saturn transit of Rohini that occurred about this time.

This means that the astronomical calendars of the Vedic people also place their texts much earlier than the 1500-1000 BCE (3500-3000 BP) period ascribed to them by Western scholars, which caused such scholars to ignore such statements as untrustworthy! In the light of the archaeology and natural history, we find that such astronomical positions are just another piece of the same fabric of evidence, pointing us in the same direction.

East to West Movement of Civilization

All ancient cultures including the Egyptian, Babylonian, Jewish, Greek and Persian saw the light of civilization and spirituality coming to them from the East. Whether it was the Egyptian sacred land of Punt in the region of the rising Sun, the Biblical Hebrews who came to the land of Ur from the East, the Persians whose Zoroastrian homeland was in Afghanistan (Bactria), the Celts who looked to teachers from Central Asia, this orientation eastward was almost universal. The idea that civilization moved from west to east is only an idea of the last few centuries.

India's connections are also to the East as we have already noted. Anyone travelling through countries like Burma, Thailand, Cambodia, Laos, Vietnam and Indonesia cannot fail to be struck by the pervasive presence of Indian culture in the region. The classical names – like Kambuja-desha (Cambodia), Champa (Vietnam), Ayutthia (for Ayodhya in Thailand), Jaya and Sumatra (in Indonesia) and many others speak of their India conneciton. The names of the greatest monuments in the region, Angkor Vat and Angkor Thom, derived from their classical Sanskrit names *Nagara-vati* and *Nagara-dhama* too tell their own story.

The two greatest ruling houses in the region were the maritime empires of the Shailendras and the Srivijayas. The Khmers of present-day Cambodia, creators of arguably the greatest civilization of the region, proudly proclaimed their Indian inspiration. Their greatest ruler was Jayavarman VII of Angkor. The kings of Thailand still call themselves Rama, the present ruler being Rama IX. The Cambodian ruler still carries the Indian royal title of Varma.

Greater Indian religion and culture drew their inspiration from India – Theravada Buddhism and Hinduism. They took the epics of the Ramayan and the Mahabharat from India, but made them their own by putting on them the stamp of their own peculiar genius. Their visual arts and performing arts bear an eloquent testimony to the inspiration of India. Their ancient deities are Indian – Shiv, Vishnu, Brahma and the Buddha. The world's greatest Vishnu mandir is found not in India, but at Angkor in Cambodia.

The plants and animals of Greater India are the same as those that flourish in India. Rice, that most characteristically East Asian food grain, sprang in Greater India and spread westward to India. The elephant, still important to the forest economy of Burma and Thailand, is the same as in India. Mandirs for the deity Ganesh are found in Thailand as they are in India. The sacred plant *ashvattha* (*Ficus religiosa*) and its platform where people gather for worship and discussion are as common there as in India.

Historians tell us that the 'Indianization' – an inelegant term, but too entrenched to change – began 2000 years ago in the southern tip of Greater India, in the region known as Funan. This is only a guess, based on scanty archaeological data and a few, mostly later, records. When we look more closely at the whole region from the Mekong and the South China Sea to the Indus and the Arabian Sea, what we see is a continuous natural zone united by climate and history. While the record for the historical period of not more than 2000 years tells us the human story of the flow of culture from India, natural history tells of a continuous exchange, which over the greater part of 20,000 years moved mainly from east to west. It was by no means all one-sided as history books portray it.

The region's greatest contribution in the post-Ice Age was probably agriculture. It began with rice cultivation in the river valleys and in the lakes fed by the mighty rivers and their tributaries to the river deltas where it has flourished ever since. Long-time maritime contacts enabled rice cultivation to spread across India, bringing about the agricultural revolution that made civilization in the region possible.

Genetic studies have shown that Indian rice varieties are related to rice grown all over Greater India. It is a similar story with agricultural livestock. The humped bull, the mainstay of Indian agriculture, and no less than a symbol of power and an object of worship, derives from the region. Beginning humbly as the domesticated variety of the regional wild cattle (*Bos banteng* or *Bos javanicus*), it made its way onto the ornate images that adorn many Harappan seals.

Figure 19: The Greater Indian Banteng and its Indian descendant on a Harappan seal

When we get to human populations, it is a similar story but with a twist. Greater Indian genetic markers appear with surprisingly high frequency in both North and South India, but Indian markers are also found in Greater India. Yet this is exactly what we would expect from the checkered history of the region and maritime contacts.

When we turn westwards from India, the scene changes dramatically. While two mighty forces — the Himalayan glaciers that feed great rivers and the monsoon rains — unite India and East Asia, high mountains and hostile deserts separate India from the west and the north. Contacts were certainly there, but they were sporadic and mainly from India going west. Contrary to scholarly views that India was populated and received the benefits of civilization from invaders from the north and west, the main movement of people and culture travelled westward out of India.

While the Western world from the time of the Greeks, if not long before, to the time of Columbus, had the idea of the fabulous wealth of India, India had no cultural history of a comparable marvelling at the West, which was generally looked down upon as a region of barbarians. There exist ample scientific, archaeological and literary records attesting to such a westward diffusion. It is also most logical. India clearly had the populations to overflow into drier Western regions.

Geneticists now hold that modern Europeans are descended from South Asians, who inhabited a region south of a line from Yemen to the Himalayas. There were two migratory routes: first a southern route through West Asia and the Levant and the Mediterranean coast; and the second, a more northerly course through Central Asia and Eurasia. These movements took place over a period of more than 10,000 years, beginning perhaps 50,000 years ago or a little less.

In this regard, there are literary accounts in the Vedas and the Purans of Indian dynasties being either driven or migrating west and north. The Ikshvaku King Mandhata (Rama's remote ancestor) drove some troublesome princes and their followers, the Druhyus, out of India to the northwest. Some time later, the Bharat King

Sudasa, assisted by the rishis Vasishtha and Vishvamitra, drove other Druhyus and the Prithu-Parthivs (proto-Persians) beyond the frontiers into Central and West Asia.

When we move to the Harappan period, records become more abundant. We have numerous Harappan artifacts including seals from Mesopotamian sites in Sumeria (Akkadia) and what is now Bahrain, which used the weights and measurements of Harappa in its trade. Indian themes like the Seated Yogi show a westward diffusion – from Harappan India, to West Asia to Celtic Europe (see figure below). Akkadian records attest to the importation of trade items like cotton and lapis lazuli (a semi-precious stone) from India.

Figure 20: The Seated Yogi (including the Pashupati) was a popular theme in the ancient world. We see it moving from Harappan India (c. 2700 BCE, 3700 BP) to West Asia (c. 2000 BCE, 4000 BP) to Celtic Europe (Denmark, c. 100 BCE, 2100 BP)

While Indian artifacts in West Asia are common, Mesopotamian artifacts in India are rare. This suggests a mainly westward movement and not a free exchange as with India and Greater India. Even in Greco-Roman times the main trade was from India, which drained the Roman economy.

With the drying up of the Sarasvati in the 2200-1900 BCE (4200-3900 BP) peri-od, followed by the decline of the Harappan civilization, there were further move-ments west out of India. A people of Indian origin known as the Kassites, went west and overthrew the Amorite Empire of Babylon (of the famous Hammurabi). Beginning about 1750 BCE (3750 BP) a Kassite military class ruled Babylon for over 500 years. Their deities – Shimalaya (Himalaya), Maruttias (Maruts), Surias (Surya) and others attest to their Indian ancestry. Some centuries later, the Hittites and the Mittanis sealed a treaty by invoking Vedic deities like Indra, Mitra and Varun in Anatolia, nearly a thousand miles to the west. These Indian people occur mainly as ruling aristocracy, not as uncivilized barbarians.

It was not until the time of Alexander the Great in the fourth century BCE (600 BP) that Western peoples finally made it to India in a significant way. Yet the Greeks did not find an uncivilized India. Instead they marvelled at its civilization and made an effort to learn from it, particularly on spiritual matters. The message is clear: the movements of peoples, culture and spirituality in ancient times were mainly from east to west.

The Spiritual Heritage of Ancient India

Ancient India has bestowed on the world one of the greatest cultural heritages of all time. The following chapter will provide more information about its nature, relevance and sophistication. *We cannot isolate India's cultural heritage from its archaeological record. Such a profound cultural heritage requires a parallel civilization in order to produce it. This is provided by the ruins of Harappan India and the Sarasvati culture.*

India's spiritual heritage is particularly profound and has given the world the Hindu, Buddhist and Jain traditions that have dominated the spiritual life of Asia and strongly impacted the rest of the world as well. These 'Indic traditions' are one of the two main religious focuses in humanity alongwith the 'Biblical traditions' of Judaism, Christianity and Islam. They have historically been followed by a larger number of people.

These Indic traditions offer humanity a different, more tolerant and generally more internal view of religion, not based on belief, dogma or history but on meditation, devotion and the eternal truth. Such a vast and diverse spiritual ethos could only have arisen as the fruit of a great ancient civilization! While these Indic traditions are not all Vedic in nature, they do reflect an India or Bharatiya concern with dharma, devotion, karma, rebirth and yogic practices aimed at developing the body and mind for the purposes of self-realization and God-realization.

For understanding human civilization, this spiritual heritage of India remains crucial and is worthy of deep study by all. Without considering it, our views, both of the world and of our human potential, are bound to be diminished.

THE LITERARY HERITAGE

What, one may ask, is the largest literature that we possess from the ancient world, through which we can still hear today the living voice of the ancient world? Is it some record from ancient Greece, Egypt or Sumeria? *No, it is the Vedic literature of India.* This Vedic voice of ancient India has continued to reverberate throughout the ages through daily chants and rituals practiced all over the country and across continents, while the voices of other ancient cultures have long fallen silent.

The greatest heritage that we have from ancient India is arguably its literary heritage, the Vedic literature. We can also call this literary heritage 'the Sarasvati heritage', because Sarasvati was not just a river but the goddess of speech and higher knowledge. This vast Vedic literature complements the extensive urban remains of the Vedic-Harappan era and gives it a voice. While ancient Egypt may have left great pyramids in stone, ancient India has left us these great Vedic pyramids of knowledge which have not gone mute with the passage of time.

In the Upanishadic era, great kings like Janak of Videha sponsored large gatherings of the sages at his capital of Mithila, which became a great centre of learning. Other ancient kings did the same, setting up a heritage of royal patronage of culture that extended into the period of classical India.

In Vedic times, great gatherings of rishis occurred at the sacred confluence of the Sarasvati and Drishadvati rivers in the Kurukshetra region, near the Harappan site of Kalibangan, hosted by the Puru and Bharat Kings. With the drying up of the Sarasvati these gatherings also shifted their location, some to the northwest in Takshashila, where a great university was formed, others to the southeast to Naimisha, Mithila and Varanasi (Benares). One old Upanishad, the Chagaleya, addresses such a gathering on the Sarasvati. We can see through such events how the Vedic literature was compiled and preserved. It formed the pillar of the entire culture.

An Overview of Vedic Literature
Vedas, Vedangs, Upavedas and Shaddarshans

It is important that we take a broad view of Vedic literature, which is quite extensive and has many sides and layers. Vedic literature itself is a compilation covering a long period of time from the early beginnings of agriculture to the urban age that preceded the Mahabharat War. It is the product of numerous seers or rishis and their families and was sustained by the support of many royal families.

The earliest of the four Vedas is the Rig Veda, which consists of around a thousand hymns or ten thousand verses. Yet the Rig Veda itself has many layers, perhaps more so than all the rest of the Vedic literature, speaking already of both ancient and modern seers going back to a remote and almost forgotten past. We can discover the foundation of Vedic culture, and the oldest record of Indian civilization, in the core ideas found in this text.

The greater Vedic corpus was compiled by Bhagwan Ved Vyas, shortly after the time of the Mahabharat War. According to Puranic lists, Ved Vyas was the twenty-eighth of such great compilers extending back to the time of Manu. This means that the existent Vedic literature we have is just the last phase of a much older literature that had already gone through several compilations.

The existent Vedic texts were gathered at the end of the Vedic period, though they reflect at least some teachings set forth at its beginning. This means that the Vedic is the heritage not just of a generation or two, but of India's ancient civilization over many thousands of years!

The Vedic tradition does not just consist of religious or spiritual knowledge. It extends to all aspects of life, from habits of daily living, to health, human relations, social sciences, physical sciences, art and music, up to all aspects of consciousness, human and universal. This is because the concern of the Vedas is with dharma or the truth of life as a whole, not just one religious identity as opposed to another.

Yet the existent texts that have been preserved reflect many more that have been lost over the course of time, including those that may be connected to non-Vedic (and pre-Vedic) traditions in India. The Vedic literature, therefore, is a good example of India's ancient civilization but much more would have existed besides it. We can use it as a doorway into ancient India's great civilization but, like archaeological ruins, is only a reflection of a much greater glory.

THE FOUR VEDAS

The four Vedas are a large collection of teachings, hymns or mantric verses which address the main powers of life, consciousness and the elements behind both the universe and the psyche. The Four Vedas are:

1. Rig Veda, 2. Yajur Veda, 3. Sama Veda and 4. Atharva Veda

The Rig Veda is the primary Veda consisting of 1017 hymns that are also the source for the mantras for the other Vedas. Its main concern is the worship of the *devtas,* starting with Agni (Fire), which represent both the great forces of nature and those of the human psyche.

The Yajur Veda has many verses in common with the Rig Veda but many of its own of a similar nature, following a more overt ritualistic approach than the Rig

Veda. It exists in several recensions as the white (Shukla) and black (Krishna).

The Sama Veda consists almost entirely of a small selection from Rig Vedic hymns but put in a more musical tonality. It is often considered to be the Veda of music or song and is highly devotional in nature.

The Atharva Veda is like a supplement to Rig Veda and adds additional hymns and mantras about a variety of human concerns from the mundane to the spiritual. It contains many verses from the Rig Veda and a few from the Yajur Veda as well as many of its own.

These four Vedas contain over two thousand hymns in the mantra portions and over three thousand pages in the prose portions. Yet there are records of many other Vedic texts and recensions that were lost, much more than what has been preserved. According to the Taittiriya Brahmana, "The Vedas are limitless".

All four Vedas are attributed to the same main Vedic Rishi families or *gotras*, like Angirasas, Bhrigus, Atharvans and Kashyapas and their offshoots as Agatsyas, Vasishthas, Gotamas, Bharadvajs, Kanwas, Atris, Vishvamitras and so on.[61] Most of the people in India today can trace their family backgrounds to such Vedic *gotras*.

These four Vedas are divided fourfold according to their different types of teachings. Besides this main hymn portion of the four Vedas are three other sections or supplements for explaining them. This makes for four aspects of Vedic literature.

1. Samhita – the main mantric portion
2. Brahmana – prose or ritualistic portion
3. Aranyaka – meditational portion
4. Upanishad – self-knowledge portion

Along with the Samhitas, the Brahmanas are the most extensive aspects of Vedic literature. Many Brahmana texts have survived, including long texts like the Taittiriya, Shatapath, Chhandogya and Aitareya that extend to hundreds of pages each.

Aranyakas and Upanishads can also be viewed as subsections of Brahmanas. The division between them is one of degree. Aranyakas and Upanishads sometimes occur in the context of Brahmanas (like the Brihadaranyak Upanishad in the Shatapath Brahmana). Upanishads also sometimes occur in the context of Aranyakas (like the Taittiriya and Mahanarayana Upanishads in the Taittiriya Aranyaka).

Overall Brahmanas deal more with the ritualistic aspect of Vedic mantras, including all aspects of Karma Yoga, as a kind of expansion of the approach of the Yajur Veda. The Aranyakas and Upanishads deal more with the deeper aspects of the Vedic hymns including spiritual knowledge, devotion to God, and yogic practices of *pranayam,* mantra and meditation. The great old Upanishads like the Brihadaranyak, Chhandogya, Taittiriya, Aitareya and Isha are the most important. Apart from these older Upanishads, are many later Upanishads not directly part of the Vedic corpus.

The Samhita itself can be interpreted as ritual (Brahmana) or spiritual knowledge (Upanishad). The mantras can be viewed in either light depending upon whether we look at them from a spiritual (*adhyatmik*) level or a material (*adhibhautik*) level. The Vedic teachings set forth a ritual that is both external (fire-offerings) and internal (offering speech, mind and *pran* into the inner fire). In this regard, the Upanishads quote great Vedic rishis for their statements of spiritual realization, including Vamadeva, Vishvamitra, Vasishtha, Agatsya, Dirghatamas, Brihaspati and Manu. The Brihadaranyak Upanishad notes:

All this in the beginning was Brahman. It knew itself as 'I am Brahman'.

The Rishi Vamadeva realized this when he said in the Rig Veda, 'I was Manu and the Sun'.

- BU I.4.10.

In addition, one must not forget the legendary fifth Veda, the Mahabharat, much of which consists of either a comment on or an expansion of Vedic ideas. The entire Vedic philosophy is eloquently summarized in the text of the Bhagvad Gita, by the greatest of the late Vedic teachers, Krishna. It remains the easiest point of access to Vedic teachings for students today.

SUPPLEMENTARY VEDIC LITERATURE

Besides these prime Vedic texts are additional supplemental Vedic texts. These explain and apply the Vedic mantras along more specific lines.

SIX VEDANGS

There are six Vedangs or 'limbs of the Veda', which provide the main tools used to properly apply the Vedic mantras.

1. Jyotish – astronomy/astrology
2. Kalpa – rules of rituals
3. Shiksha – pronunciation
4. Vyakran – grammar
5. Nirukta – etymology
6. Chhandas – poetic metres

Jyotish provided the rules for developing calendars and timing actions so that what we attempt remains in harmony with the higher powers of the universe. It is the basis of Vedic astronomy and astrology, showing how observant of the heavens the Vedic people were. The Vedic mantras themselves were seen as reflecting the cosmic movement of time.

The last four of the Vedangs relate specifically to the study of language and mantra. This shows the esteem held by language studies in ancient India and forms the basis of what we can call 'Vedic linguistics'. Vedic teachers analyzed sounds and words to a very subtle level, proposing the cosmic vibration OM as the origin of all sound and language. It was not just a question of human speech but understanding the language of nature and the Word of God. This profound study of language and sound also allowed them to preserve the Vedas according to strict rules of pronunciation and tonality.

SANSKRIT AND ITS HERITAGE

India's greatest gift to mankind is probably the Sanskrit language, which remains by many accounts both the most spiritual and scientific of all languages. It is the very language of the deities and of mantra – spiritual speech.

The Vedic language was mainly based on metres or *chhandas*. We can call this *chhandas* language the Vedic Sarasvati language. The Vedas also represent the largest collection of poetry from the ancient world. Such a sophisticated metrical language also shows a high intellectual culture among the Vedic people.

Classical Sanskrit was structured by the great grammarian Panini in the post-Vedic era. Yet even he looks back to many other grammarians and Vedic linguists before his time. The great Vedic Rishi Dirghatamas states in the Rig Veda:

On the imperishable syllable of the chant in the Supreme Ether of the heart, all the Gods reside. Those who don't know this, what can they do with the chant?

- RV I.164.39

To really understand the Vedas we must, through Yoga and *sadhana* and the study of mantra, go back to its spiritual meaning. Few scholars in the West have even considered this possibility, resting their interpretations on mundane factors only.

FOUR UPAVEDAS

Along with the Vedangs, four Upavedas or secondary Vedic texts address the following topics:

1. Ayurveda – Vedic science of living
2. Dhanurveda – martial arts
3. Sthapatya Veda – architecture, sculpture and geomancy
4. Gandharva Veda – music, poetry and dance

Ayurveda became the basis of Indian medicine, combining all three – physical, psychological and spiritual – aspects. It was later adapted by Buddhist, Jain and other non-Vedic schools as well. Its three *doshas* or three humour theory has its origin in the three great Vedic deities of Indra (air), Agni (fire) and Soma (water).

Dhanurveda developed into many forms of martial arts, diplomacy and state-craft. It was part of the Vedic Raja Dharma or the duty of kings.

Sthapatya Veda developed into Vastu or the Vedic directional science for proper orientation of buildings and houses. Mandir building in ancient India developed out of Sthapatya Veda, arising from the models of Vedic fire altars and chariots.

Gandharva Veda, along with the Sama Veda, became the basis of India's great traditions of music, dance, drama, poetry and literature.

In addition to lost Vedas and Brahmanas, there is a record of many other ancient texts that have been lost, including works on grammar, astronomy, medicine, art and dance - that relate to all the Vedangs and Upavedas. This means that even this massive body of preserved Vedic literature is just a remnant of a much larger original Vedic corpus, just as the existent urban ruins of ancient India are remnants of a vaster and more detailed culture.

THE SIX SCHOOLS OF VEDIC PHILOSOPHY

Out of the Vedas arose six schools of philosophy, *shad darshans*, which literally means six ways of seeing or insight. They were designed to show the logical, metaphysical and cosmological implications that could be found within the Vedic mantras.

The Six Schools of Vedic Philosophy and Their Founders:

1. Nyay – Logic School – founded by Gautam
2. Vaisheshik – Atomic School – founded by Kanad
3. Samkhya – Cosmic Principle School – founded by Kapila
4. Yoga – Yoga School – founded by Hiranyagarbha and Patanjali
5. Purva Mimamsa – Ritualistic School – founded by Jaimini
6. Uttar Mimamsa/Vedant – Theological or Metaphysical School – founded by Ved Vyas (Badarayana)

Gautam's Nyay system provides one of the oldest systems of logical philosophy in the world, showing the principles of clear thinking and critical examination from a rational and experiential standpoint.

Vaisheshik introduces an atomic theory for the first time in world thought, reflecting the Vedic idea that the Self is smaller than the smallest particle. It also organizes our experience according to certain cosmic principles and shows us how to think categorically.

Samkhya explains the main principles behind the creation of the universe from primal matter called Prakriti to the five elements, as overseen by the consciousness factor of the Purush in the form of twenty-five key principles. It outlines a means to realize the Purush or higher Self and gain liberation or Kaivalya through knowledge of these principles.

Yoga outlines a practical method of realization of the Self or Purush through eight limbs or practices: *yam* (disciplines), *niyam* (observances), *asana* (physical postures), *pranayam* (control of life forces through breath), *pratyahar* (control of the senses), *dharana* (concentration), *dhyan* (meditation) and *samadhi* (realization). It adds a special emphasis on Ishvar or deity along with the Purush principle of Samkhya. Patanjali's *Yoga Sutras* is simply a compilation of yogic principles going back to very ancient times.

Purva Mimamsa explains the Vedic science of ritual for achieving the goals of human life, mundane and spiritual. It shows how our actions link up with cosmic forces and spiritual influences and can be organized consciously to make our lives function more smoothly and effectively.

Uttar Mimamsa, also called Vedant, provides the metaphysics and theology for the Vedic search for self-realization. It posits Brahman or Being-Consciousness-Bliss as the Supreme Reality behind the universe and the ultimate goal of human life. It is prior historically to and more sophisticated than Western theological thought developed through Greek and Christian thinkers.

All later philosophies of India owe a great deal to this Vedic philosophical foundation and most consist of variations upon its formulations. These six schools also overlap and share a lot in common. For example, a ground in the logical thinking through the study of Nyay and Vaisheshik was considered necessary to approach the other schools as well. The disciplines of Yoga were also adopted by all the schools. The goal of self-knowledge or *moksha* was the highest goal of all schools.

No other ancient civilization has preserved and passed on such a deep spiritual and philosophical tradition, with so many great teachers and teachings over such a long period of time. Ancient Western philosophy through the Greeks, though it started much later than the Hindu, has long passed into obscurity. Whereas, Vedic traditions, particularly Vedant, remain alive and vibrant and form the mainstream of philosophical thinking in India to the present day.

While Western philosophy fell from an earlier spiritual basis in the Greeks into materializm, Indian philosophy has maintained both its spiritual orientation as well as its *sadhanas* to reach the higher consciousness that the philosophy envisions. Modern Vedantic teachers like Swami Vivekanand, Sri Aurobindo, Ramana Maharshi, Chinmayanand Swami or Pramukh Swami Maharaj show the power of this Vedantic tradition that is still engaging some of the greatest minds in the world, including many modern scientists.

VEDA AND DHARMA

The main focus of Indic thought has always been the concept of dharma. Dharma is one of those terms that is really not possible to translate. It refers to the natural laws that uphold the universe, including physical, mental and spiritual principles of right and appropriate action. The Vedas exist primarily to teach dharma or the right way of living on all levels of our being. There is a family dharma, the proper relationship of husband and wife, parents and children. There is the social dharma, the proper relationship of the different groups, classes and strata of society. There is a spiritual dharma, the pursuit of *moksha* or the liberation of the spirit. There is a dharmic way to do everything in harmony with the greater universe of consciousness and with respect for all living beings.

All the spiritual traditions of India aim at dharma from different angles and are therefore called 'dharmic traditions'. Buddhism called itself Buddha Dharma, Jainism as Jain Dharma, and Sikhism as Sikh Dharma. The different *sampradays* of Hinduism or Sanatan Dharma have also defined themselves as Shaiv Dharma, Shakta Dharma, Vaishnav Dharma and so on.

This dharmic view of the world is another key heritage from ancient India. The term dharma first arises in the Rig Veda: 'By the truth upholding the foundational truth, in the power of the Offering in the supreme ether, the seers reached the deities who are seated in the Dharma that upholds heaven." RV V.15.2. This realization of dharma at the highest level is what creates the status of the rishi. In the Rig Veda the term Dharma is used along with the terms *ritam,* cosmic law, *satyam,* universal truth, and *brihat,* vast, lofty or unlimited.

The term dharma itself becomes very common in later Vedic literature, where there is an entire category of Dharma Sutras. Many of these, like the Manu Smriti, deal with the daily rules of personal and family life and societal conduct. Such a well codified, ceremonial and highly ritualized life, as shown in this greater Vedic literature, reflects very old and intricate customs of an advanced civilization.

YAGNA, THE WAY OF OFFERING

The Vedic, like many ancient traditions, speaks of 'offering' as the underlying principle of life. The ancients perceived a sacred order behind all the movements of life, with each creature serving as an offering to the entire universe and the entire universe providing a support in return for each creature.

The Vedic term is *yagna*. *Yagna* means to offer, give, worship and unify. *Yagnas* include not only fire offerings, the common outward offering ritual, but also internal practices of prayer, mantra, *pranayam* and meditation. In other words, there are not only outer offerings but inner offerings of our own being to the Divine.

There are five daily *yagnas* as outlined in the Brahmanas:

Brahma Yagna – Study and teaching the Vedas or sacred teachings

Deva Yagna – Worshipping the Divine and the cosmic powers

Manushya Yagna – Helping fellow human beings, particularly taking care of guests

Pitri Yagna – Honouring one's ancestors

Bhuta Yagna – Serving living beings, making offerings to animals and other creatures

Reflecting this emphasis on dharma, the ancient literature of India has left us with certain important values about life. These Vedic values are perhaps the most important and enduring aspect of the Vedic heritage. A good view of these can be found in the Vedic hymn to the Earth.

Satyam brihad rtam ugram diksha tapo brahma yagnah prthivim dharayanti

Sa no bhutasya bhavyasya patni urum lokam prthivi nah krnotu

Truth, vastness, order, power, consecration, discipline, prayer and offering uphold the Earth: May She, the queen of what has been and what will be, may the Earth grant us a wide space.

- AV XII.1

Science in Ancient India

One of the basic Western assumptions about the ancient Hindus is that they were not of a scientific bent of mind and their contribution to the history of science is negligible. While this is another colonial prejudice, it has left its mark on the minds of many people, even though Indian scientists are now famous throughout the world!

A different picture begins to emerge when competent scientists start to examine Indian achievements in science and technology. An examination of the great cities, harbours and citadels of the Harappan Civilization show its creators to have been highly skilled city planners, engineers and architects. A closer examination reveals no less an impressive mastery of metallurgy, mathematics and other sciences. Steel was an Indian invention. And, until the fifteenth century, India was ahead of Europeans in mathematics.

Major mathematical concepts like the zero and the use of the decimal system are now known to have been first invented in India. The idea of zero goes back to the Upanishads and the Vedas, which identify Brahman or the supreme reality with space and with the supreme ether (*param vyom*) of the Vedas.

As early as the Yajur Veda (SYV VII.2), a sequence of numbers is indicated from one to one followed by twelve zeroes (1,000,000,000,000):

These, O Agni, are my bricks that yield sustenance, one (*eka*) and a ten (*dasa*), ten and a hundred (*sata*), a hundred and a thousand (*sahasram*), a thousand and ten thousand (*ayuta*), ten thousand and a hundred thousand (*niyuta*), a hundred thousand and a million (*prayu-tam*), a million and ten million (*arbudam*), a hundred million (*nyarbudam*), a billion (*samudra*), ten billion (*madhyam*), a hundred billion (*antas*) and a thousand billion (*parardha*).

Indian achievements in science were famous throughout the world. Medieval and ancient scholars from Arabia, Spain, China and even Greece acknowledged their indebtedness to Indian science. A medieval Arab scholar Sa'id ibn Ahmad al-Andalusi (1029-1070) wrote in his *Tabaqat al-'umam,* one of the earliest books on the history of the sciences:

> The first nation to have cultivated science is India. ...India is known for the wisdom of its people. Over many centuries, all the kings of the past have recognized the ability of the Indians in all the branches of knowledge.
>
> The kings of China have stated that the kings of the world are five in number and all the people of the world are their subjects. They mentioned the king of China, the king of India, the king of the Turks, the king of the Persians, and the king of the Romans.
>
> ...They referred to the king of India as the "king of wisdom" because of the Indians' careful treatment of *'ulum* [sciences] and all the branches of knowledge.
>
> The Indians, known to all nations for many centuries, are the metal [essence] of wisdom, the source of fairness and objectivity. They are people of sublime pensiveness, universal apologues, and useful and rare inventions.
>
> ...To their credit the Indians have made great strides in the study of numbers and of geometry. They have acquired immense information and reached the zenith in their knowledge of the movements of the stars [astronomy] ...After all that they have surpassed all other peoples in their knowledge of medical sciences...

When modern European scholars were claiming that Indian mathematics was borrowed from the Greeks, as far back as 662 CE, Sebokht, the Bishop of Qinnesrin in North Syria had observed:

I will omit all discussion of the science of the Hindus [Indians], a people not the same as Syrians, their subtle discoveries in the science of astronomy, *discoveries more ingenious than those of the Greeks and the Babylonians;* their valuable method of calculation; their computing that surpasses description. I wish only to say that this computation is done by means of nine signs.

Sebokht, like most learned men of the day, was thoroughly familiar with Greek learning and found Indian mathematics to be far superior. The system of computing that he mentions, which "surpasses description" is of course the decimal place value system or the modern number system that we use today. Many scientific thinkers consider the invention of the modern number system the greatest invention ever made by man. Without it modern civilization would be impossible. In his three-volume work *The Universal History of Numbers,* the French-Moroccan scholar Georges Ifrah waxes lyrical in describing the achievement:

Finally it all came to pass as though across the ages and the civilizations, the human mind had tried all the possible solutions to the problem of writing numbers, before universally adopting the one which seemed the most abstract, the most perfected and the most effective of all. ...The measure of genius of the Indian civilization, to which we owe our modern system, is all the greater in that it was the only one in all history to have achieved this triumph.

Computers today use the binary system, which was also known to Vedic thinkers. Pingal who wrote an important work on Vedic poetics, which classifies metrical syllables in a binary way as long or short, showed how to count using the binary system thousands of years ago. The famous grammarian Panini was by tradition Pingal's brother. Computer scientists today are finding Panini's highly scientific approach to language and linguistics valuable in designing computer languages.

Meanwhile, Baudhayan, in his *Shulba Sutras* of the late Vedic age, outlined geometry for the construction of mandirs and large buildings, long before the Greeks worked out their theories in the field. Noted Western mathematician Seidenberg saw the Vedic *Shulba Sutras* as the basis of Babylonian and Egyptian mathematics. [62]

What set Indian science back was the extremely unsettled conditions in Medieval India beginning in about the tenth century. Now that India is free again, Indians are reasserting their excellence in science and technology.

VEDIC ASTRONOMY

Astronomy was another subject in which Indians excelled and merits a special study in its own right. Jean-Sylvan Bailey, a nineteenth century French astronomer, was amazed by the accuracy of the tables compiled by ancient Indians. He observed:

> ...the motions of the stars calculated by the Hindus before some 4500 years vary not even a
> single minute from the tables of Cassine and Meyer {used in Europe in the nineteenth cen-
> tury]. The Indian tables give the same annual variation of the moon as that discovered by
> Tycho Brahe – a variation unknown to the school of Alexandria and also to the Arabs who
> followed the calculations of the school. ...*The Hindu systems of astronomy are by far the oldest and
> that from which the Egyptians, Greeks, Romans and even the Jews derive their knowledge.*

SPEED OF LIGHT

Noted scientist Subhash Kak has pointed out an accurate calculation occurring in commentaries to Vedic texts.[63] The Vedic commentator, Sayana, in the fourteenth century notes in Rig Veda I.50, a hymn to the Sun.

Tatha ca smaryate yojananam sahasre dve dve sata dve ca yojane ekena misardhena kra-mamana

Thus it is remembered, O Sun you who traverse 2002 *yojans* in half a *nimesh*.

A *nimesh* is about 1/5 of a second. A *yojan* is about 9 miles. This provides a figure very close to the 186,000 miles per second of the speed of light.

THE ZODIAC OF 360 DEGREES

Another important mathematical invention on par with the decimal system is the idea of a circle of 360 degrees used for astronomical purposes. This too we first find in Vedic texts, long before the Babylonians used it in the fourth century BCE (2400 BP). The Rig Veda speaks of a wheel of heaven of 360 or 720 divisions.

> 11. The wheel of law with 12 spokes does not decay as it revolves around heaven. Oh Fire, here your 720 sons abide in pairs.
>
> 12. The Father with 5 feet and 12 forms, they say, dwells in the higher half of heaven full of waters. Others say that he is the clear-seeing one who dwells below in a sevenfold wheel that has six spokes.
>
> 48. Twelve are its fellies. The wheel is one. It has three naves. Who has understood it?
> In it they are held together like the 360 spokes, both moving and non-moving.
>
> > - RV I.164.

Various divisions of this 360-spoke wheel of Heaven are indicated including one by twelve, which reflects the idea of the 12 signs of the zodiac.

The Shatapath Brahmana X.5.5, a late Vedic text, also speaks of a wheel of heaven with 720 divisions. "But indeed that Fire-altar is also the *nakshatras*. For there are twenty-seven of these *nakshatras* and twenty-seven secondary *nakshatras*.

This makes 720." Note that twenty-seven times twenty-seven *nakshatras* equals 729, with which some overlap, can be related to the 720 half-degrees of the zodiac. We see from such passages that the Vedic rishis had a profound mathematical knowledge and a keen observation of small portions of the sky.

THE NAKSHATRAS

The Vedic rishis perceived spiritual and karmic influences coming from the stars and planets. This gave their astronomy an astrological side as well. They mapped out the spiritual influences of the stars in their *nakshatra* system of 27 or 28 lunar constellations.

The Taittiriya Brahmana lists in details the influences of the *nakshatras* on human behaviour and what each *nakshatra* is good for. It says that after death the human soul can go to the regions of these *nakshatras* and the deities which rule them.

COSMIC TIME CYCLES

The Rig Veda (IV.58.3) speaks of the cosmic bull with "four horns, three feet, two heads and seven hands." This refers to the *kalpa* number 4,320,000,000, the great age in Vedic astronomy. The Atharva Veda (VIII.21) also mentions *yugas* of 10,000 years in length, "ten thousand, two *yugas*, three *yugas*, four *yugas*." The Vedic people were aware of such long time cycles that included eras before the flood and the current Manu or age of humanity.

PLANETS AND SIGNS OF THE ZODIAC

Vedic texts refer to planets or *grahas*, *rashis* or signs and eclipses. The Rig Veda, while indicating a wheel of heaven of 360 spokes, speaks of its division into twelve parts, suggesting the twelve signs of the zodiac. The Taittiriya Brahmana states that the creator when creating the stars gave each an animal.

In the Aitareya Brahmana, the planets Venus (Bhrigu) and Jupiter (Brihaspati) were said to have been born of the seed of the Creator Prajapati, who is identified astronomically with the *nakshatra* Mrigashirsha or Orion, which marks the region of the sky where the Milky Way crosses the zodiac in the north.

The Atharva Veda mentions the *grahas* (planets) and Rahu, the eclipse causing lunar nodes, "Peaceful for us be the planets and the Moon, peaceful the Sun and Rahu (AV XIX.9.10)." *Graha* is the Hindu astronomical term for a planet. The same hymn (v.7) says the *grahas* "move in Heaven". Should we have any doubt that it is the planets they refer to? Rahu is the north lunar node. Knowledge of the lunar nodes suggests the capacity to predict eclipses, as it is through them that knowledge of the nodes arises. The importance of eclipses as omens in ancient cultures is well known from literature all over the world and they were also probably used to help determine the calendar.

There are different Vedic deities for the Sun at different times of the day, the different seasons of the year (7) and the different months of the year (12). Vedic texts like the Taittiriya Brahmana describe different names explaining the different qualities for the different days and nights of the lunar month, both waxing and waning, reflecting a deep understanding of the forces of time.

Vastu and Directional Influences

The Atharva Veda III.27 mentions the directional influences that along with some variation and expansion over time became the basis of Vastu. It places Agni or fire in the east, Indra in the south, Varun in the west, Soma in the north, Vishnu in the centre and Brihaspati on the top.

AYURVEDA – THE VEDIC SCIENCE OF LIFE

Ayurvedic medicine, another important gift of Vedic knowledge, deserves more detailed mention as well. The main concepts of Ayurveda can be found in the Rig Veda. The three main deities in the Rig Veda of Indra, Vata or Vayu (air), Agni and Surya (fire and the sun) and Soma (water or the moon), correspond to the three *doshas* or biological humours of Ayurveda as *vata, pitta* and *kapha.*

The Rig Veda refers to healing mixtures of plant juices, milk, yogurt, honey, ghee and soma and refers to several of its deities as great physicians including the twin Ashvins, Rudra and Soma. Rudra is said to be the greatest of the physicians. "Rudra, we know you as the foremost physician among physicians (RV II.33.4)."

The Yajur Veda specifically mentions the main tissues and organs of the body. It says that long life is one of the main fruits that can be gained through the performance of the Vedic Offering or *yagna.* The Atharva Veda speaks of the healing powers of specific plants and outlines the use of Vedic mantras to treat various diseases.

Later important historical Ayurvedic physicians include Dhanvantari of Kashi, Charak and Sushrut. Charak and Sushrut created schools which have left us extensive medical collections, such as *Charak Samhita* and *Sushrut Samhita* that are among the oldest and most comprehensive in the world. In the Rig Veda itself, the hymns of Kakshivin to the Ashvins (I.116-119) speak of many miraculous actions including the use of artificial limbs, restoration of sight to the blind, and even bringing back people from the dead.

THE ANCIENT VEDIC YOGA

Yoga is probably the most characteristic practice of India's spiritual traditions. We find it pervading all domains of Indic thought and culture. Aspects of Yoga – which include yoga postures, *pranayam,* ritual, mantra and meditation – can be found in Indian music, dance, medicine, martial arts, and in all its spiritual traditions, Vedic and non-Vedic. Yoga is one of India's greatest gifts to humanity.

Yoga is a Sanskrit word meaning union. More specifically, it refers to the proper coordination of factors to reach a specific result or aim, which spiritually speaking is the harmonizing of our inner nature for the purpose of self-realization and God-realization. Yoga originally arose in the context of Vedic mantras and symbolizm. Yoga is the practice of which Vedic knowledge provides the theory.

The earliest specific references to Yoga occur in Vedic literature, as the following verse, which originally comes from the Rig Veda but also occurs in the Yajur Veda and Upanishads.

Yunjante mana uta yunjante dhiyo vipra viprasya brihato vipascittah

Seers of the vast illumed seer yogically control their minds and intellects.

- RV V.81.1, SYJ XI.4, Svestasvatara Upanishad II.1

Patanjali in his famous *Yogasutra* defines Yoga as *'yogashcitta vritti-nirodha'* (i.e. Yoga is the control of the natural tendencies of the mind), echoing the same idea.

Yet many other Vedic terms can be synonyms for Yoga in various contexts or from various angles. These include mantra, *upasana, yagna, tapas* and *dhyan*. Once we accept the yogic implication of these key Vedic terms and practices, then it is easy to see that some form of Yoga pervades all aspects of Vedic culture. In the later literature many Vedic rishis are also famous as great yogis and even have such names as Vasishtha, Parashar, Bharadvaj, Agatsya, Yagnavalkya, Asit and Deval Kashyap. Some even have Yoga postures named after them.

We can probably best understand the practice of Yoga as an inner offering (*antar yagna*). This is also how it is explained in the fourth chapter of the Bhagvad Gita. Note that the term Yoga is a very common term in the Gita and Krishna is lauded as the great original teacher of Yoga, who taught Yoga even to Manu and Ikshvaku, the first king. Manu's connection with Yoga suggests that Yoga was a tradition carried on from pre-Ice Age cultures.

As an inner *yagna* or offering, we can also explain Yoga as a balancing of Agni and Soma or the powers of fire and water within the psyche. In Yogic and Vedic thought, Agni relates to the lower *chakras* and the ascending Kundalini Fire. Soma relates to the crown *chakra* and the descending nectar or Amrit. Indra is the power of the third eye or Ajna *chakra* which energizes this process.

Of the specific branches of Yoga, most have their counterparts in Vedic texts.

Mantra Yoga in particular finds its roots in Vedic mantras like OM and Vedic verses like the Gayatri and Mahamrityunjay mantras. In fact the Vedas can be seen as entirely texts of Mantra Yoga.

Karma Yoga is contained in the Vedic ritualistic approach to life and in Vedic concepts of charity (*dana*), offering (*yagna*). The Brahmanas outline five great offerings as part of one's daily actions. These are as previously noted on page 139.

Bhakti Yoga is the most common approach in the Vedic hymns that speak of the Divine as the father, mother, brother, sister, friend and beloved. All the main attitudes (*bhav*) of devotion can be found in the Rig Veda itself. As a hymn to Indra states, "Thou, O Indra, are our father and thou are our mother, Shatakratu. Hence we implore your grace (RV VIII.98.11)." It included a common practice of chanting divine names or names of the deities. "All partake of the Divine Name, following the immortal truth according to their ways."

- RV I.68.2

Gnan Yoga or the Yoga of Knowledge exists in the Vedic emphasis on meditation, light and insight. "Declaring the truth, meditating directly, the sons of Heaven, the heroes of the Almighty, holding the station of seers, the Angirasas thought out the original nature of the Offering (RV X.67.2)." Vedic mantras themselves were to be meditated upon.

Pran Yoga occurs in the primacy of deities of Pran and Vayu (air) like Indra, the Maruts and Shiv. Vedic mantras were also used for counting the breath in the practice of *pranayam*.

This spiritual legacy of Yoga is perhaps ancient India's greatest contribution to world civilization and one that shows the depth and profundity of its culture.

Postscript: Continued Development

Out of the matrix of the vast and many-sided teachings, such as we see in the Vedas, other traditions, Vedic and non-Vedic, arose over time. As the region fostered tolerance and continuity, the various Indic traditions, Vedic and non-Vedic, coexisted, intermingled and interacted through time and continued to share much in common, following the dharmic view of the world that characterizes the soul of India.

While the Vedic remains the oldest preserved *dharmic* tradition, it has also changed over time and interacted with other traditions, undergoing various internal and external developments. The Jain tradition is similarly quite old and looks back to kings of the Bharat era for its earliest teachers like Rishabhdev. The Buddhist tradition relates primarily to the late ancient period but refers to Buddhas earlier than the Gautam Buddha of history, like the Buddha Kashyap said to have lived 5000 years before him. Other ancient traditions like the Ajivakas have not survived the course of time. Different Hindu *sampradays* like the Shaivite, Vaishnav, Shakti, Ganapata and Saura lines have remained together under the broader umbrella of Sanatan Dharma, with a great deal of overlap as well.

The great heritage of learning started in the Vedic age continued into later India. After the Vedic age, the centre of civilization in India moved from the Sarasvati-Drishadvati region to the Ganga-Yamuna region, but also spread throughout India and all of Asia. The Vedas did not result in a dark age but in the arising of the classical civilization of India that carried the Vedic impulse to new heights and in many directions.

Vedic centres of learning like Takshashila continued to flourish. Takshashila became what is probably the world's first university and one that covered all subjects from the most profound spiritual philosophies to practical sciences and beautiful arts. Similar colleges and centres of learning occurred in Ujjain, Vikramshila, Mithila, Nalanda, Varanasi and many other great cities in India.

Vedic spirituality that had come forth through the Upanishads blossomed further through the Bhagvad Gita, the systems of Samkhya and Yoga and the many schools of Vedantic philosophy. Non-Vedic schools like Buddhism and Jainism developed similar ideas of karma, rebirth and the seeking of liberation or nirvana through meditation. Buddhist and Hindu schools spread throughout Asia and Buddhism came to dominate China and Japan. Yoga diversified into many schools and branches, creating various traditions of yogis and *siddhas* throughout the country. Vedant gave rise to profound philosophies through Shankar, Ramanuj, Madhva, Nimbark, Vallabh, Chaitanya Mahaprabhu and Swaminarayan.

Vedic literature gave way to the Puranic literature with 18 major Purans and 29 known minor Purans explaining all the secrets of the worship of the deities, Yoga, meditation and mantra as well as the rules for organizing society and ruling a kingdom. The great Mahabharat was composed, gathering all the knowledge and arts reflecting the end of the Vedic Age. The Ramayan was written by Valmiki creating the model for the epic poem that came to dominate Asia, reflecting the life of Bhagwan Ram, one of the early Vedic kings of the solar dynasty. Sanskrit literature, poetry and drama blossomed in the great works of Kalidas, Bhasa and other great poets, while Bharat Muni set forth the traditions of dance in his *Natya Shastra*.

The Vedic emphasis on mathematics continued through great mathematicians of later times like Aryabhatta and Bhaskaracharya. The Vedic knowledge of astronomy and astrology gave rise to Varahmihir and the great school of the *Brihat Parashara Hora Shastra*.

Ayurveda took shape in its own right in the compilations of Charak and Sushrut, becoming a vast medical system using herbs, drugs, surgery, psychology and an elaborate system of diagnosis and treatment of disease, with great hospitals throughout the country.

The Vedic emphasis on creating special Somas gave way to alchemical traditions through Nagarjun and other *siddhas*.

In short, as befitting such a great cultural foundation as that of the Vedic Sarasvati, later India would flower and blossom in all aspects of life and culture as an offering to the highest Divinity that dwells within us. That Vedic legacy remains the most vibrant and characteristic aspect of India's civilization.

CONTINUATION TODAY

The great cultural heritage that began with ancient India and its great rishis continues to the present day. Indic traditions continue to develop and are not averse to changing with the times, adapting their outer forms and expression but preserving their eternal truths. Though there is respect for ancient texts, the word of the living guru is equally honoured. Some modern Hindus look to their gurus rather than to a particular traditional *sampraday* for their identity. In this way many new branches of Sanatan Hindu Dharma have emerged – from Buddhism and Shikhism to recent movements of the last century like Ramakrishna Mission, Divine Life Society and others.

The Swaminarayan Sampraday began in the late eighteenth century, founded in Gujarat by Bhagwan Swaminarayan, worshipped as Parabrahma Purushottam. It is today one of the most rapidly growing *sampradays* of Hindu Dharma.

Indian gurus since Ramakrishna and Vivekanand have gained significant followings in the Western world. Other important figures now known in the West include Yoganand, Raman Maharshi, Sri Aurobindo, Swami Shivanand, Pramukh Swami Maharaj, Anandamayi Ma and Satya Sai Baba. The great cultural seeds that arose in ancient India continue to spread and flower throughout the entire world.

The Need for a New Look at Ancient India

After having gone through our book, we hope that the reader now sees the need for a new look at ancient India, and for discarding the old, now disproved false opinions. While most non-European cultures have revised their histories in the post-colonial, post-communist era that we live in today, modern India unfortunately has not done this, though it has an even older historical tradition of its own. Even the textbooks in Indian schools uncritically repeat outdated European colonial and Marxist views that reflect little understanding of the Indian mind and little respect for its dharmic culture. They also do not take into consideration recent discoveries of archaeology, geology or genetics, like the many new archaeological discoveries in India or the remapping of the Sarasvati River.

Instead they emphasize Western theories from Marxism to Freudian psychology and modern linguistics, imposing them on ancient texts and teachings and not looking at them directly in their own light. These end up telling us more about trends in modern thought than they help us to understand the ancient world and its many spiritual secrets.

It is time for India to reclaim its own history and its own legacy as a great world civilization, with due respect for the history and legacy of the other cultures but not subordinate to them. This Indian or Bharatiya legacy is that of the ancient rishi culture and the modern yogis who continue to embody it today. This is the India and Indian heritage that the world finds most appealing and engaging and that the world so desperately needs today for its own spiritual rebirth in this age of materializm and fundamentalizm.

Yet reclaiming India's past is not just an academic or even a cultural endeavour. It cannot be done only by writing better accounts of history. It requires bringing the spirit of India's great past, which is timeless, back to life today in the hearts and minds of all. It means reviving India's heritage as a means of building a greater future for the country and for the world – a future that honours the spiritual heritage of humanity that began long before and reached great heights prior to the dominance of what we call civilization and its material gains.

Our journey through history is of no value unless it helps awaken that rishi spirit within you. May you take that heritage and develop it according to your highest capacity!

SUMMARY

In summary, natural history, archaeology and ancient records give us a coherent picture of ancient India and her civilization. The ending of the last Ice Age more than 10,000 years ago released two mighty forces of nature – the Himalayan rivers of which the Sarasvati was the greatest and a more abundant monsoon. This allowed the people of greater India, once confined to coastal regions and lakes to move to the Sarasvati heartland and create the Vedic civilization that dominated the post-Ice Age period. Its gifts in language, literature, science and spirit are still with us.

The Vedic Sarasvati went through many vicissitudes and during the later phases sustained what we call the Harappan civilization. It gave us the Vedantic tradition, traces of which we find in its archaeological remains, and which is preserved in the literature that still survives to the present in the lineage of gurus and sages.

CONCLUDING MESSAGE

This brings us to the end of our journey... a ten thousand year spiritual voyage through space and time, spanning the cycle of history that began with the ending of the last Ice Age. There were such cycles before and there will be such cycles in the future. This is what our ancient rishis called *yugas*. Civilizations rise up and decay but certain values are eternal. Sanatan Dharma is the embodiment of these eternal values. It is a body of knowledge that has sustained peoples and civilizations through hardships and crises that are part of life on this planet.

Indian Culture has not only inspired and influenced great visible monuments and civilizations but also sustained the invisible, perennial stream of spiritual strength necessary for the survival of people. It seems the people of Kambuja Desha (Cambodia) survived the rapacity of colonization and the genocidal horrors of the Khmer Rogue largely on the strength of the spiritual gift they received from India. Colonization and the killing fields are long gone, but the spiritual heritage still remains. The millennial monument, the great Angkor Wat, continues to awe and inspire us.

Angkor Vat in Cambodia

Swaminarayan Akshardham in New Delhi

Similarly, as you look at the great Swaminarayan Akshardham, try to see beyond its physical magnificence and presence to catch a glimpse of the eternal spirit that made it possible. Every millennium, every *yuga*, has its challenges. And each throws up its *yuga-purush* who can lead the age and transform it.

As Shri Krishna said in the Gita (4.1)

Imam vivasvate yogam proktavanahamvyayam,

Vivasvanmanave praha manurikshvakavebravit.

That lineage continues today in Pramukh Swami Maharaj and the BAPS Swaminarayan Sanstha that he now guides. This invisible inspiration is the eternal force that created the Swaminarayan Akshardham that stands before us, timelessly representing India's past, present and future.

Bibliography

Original works cited

Amarakosa

Astadhyayi (of Panini)

Atharvaveda

Baudhayana Shulba Sutra

Mahabharat (of Krsnadvaipayana Vyasa)

Manudharma Sastra (Manu Samhita)

Matsya Purana

Pancavimsa Brahmana

Ramayan (of Valmiki)

Rigveda (Rk Samhita)

Satapatha Brahmana

Taittiriya Brahmana

Upanisads

Yajurveda (Taittiriya Samhita and *Vajasaneya Samhita)*

References

al-Andalusi, Sa'id. 1991. *Science in the Medieval World: Book of the categories of nations.* Translated and edited by S.I. Salem and Alok Kumar. University of Texas. Austin, Texas.

Aurobindo, Sri. 1991. *On the Mahabharat.* Pondicherry: Sri Aurobindo Ashram.

M. Bamshad, T. Kivisild, W.S. Watkins, M.E. Dixon, C.E. Ricker, B.B. Rao, J.M. Naidu,

B.V.R. Prasad, P.G. Reddy, A. Rasanagam, et al. 'Genetic Evidence on the Origin of Indian Caste Populations.' 2001, *Genome Research* 11, pp 994 – 1004.

Bhagwan Singh. 1995. *The Vedic Harappans.* New Delhi: Aditya Prakashan.

Bodmer, Walter and Robin McKie. 1994. *The Book of Man: The Quest to Discover Our Genetic Heritage.* London: Abacus, p 225.

Chand, Devi. 1988. *The Yajurveda* (Sanskrit text with English translation and notes). New Delhi: Munshiram Manoharlal.

Cavalli-Sforza, L.L and F. 1995. *The Great Human Diasporas.* Reading, MA: Addison-Wesley.

Cavalli-Sforza, L.L 2001. *Genes, Peoples and Languages.* Penguin.

Danino, Michel. 2001. *The Invasion that Never Was.* Mysore: Mira Aditi Center.

Datta, B.B. 1993. *Ancient Hindu Geometry: Science of the Sulba.* New Delhi: Cosmo. Emeneau, Murray. 1954. Linguistic prehistory of India. *Proceedings of the American Philosophical Society,* vol. 98, pp 282-92. Philadelphia.

Feuerstein, Georg, Subhash Kak and David Frawely. 1995. *In Search of the Cradle of Civilization.* Wheaton, Illinois: Quest Books.

Francfort, Paul-Henri. 1992. Evidence for the Harappan irrigation system in Haryana and Rajasthan. *Eastern Anthropologist* 45: 87-103.

Frawley, David. 1991. *Gods, Sages and Kings.* Twin Lakes, Wisconsin: Lotus Press. (Indian edition by Motilal-Banarsidass, New Delhi)

Frawley, David. 1994. *Myth of the Aryan Invasion.* New Delhi, Voice of India.

Frawley, David. 2001. *The Rig Veda and the History of India.* New Delhi, Aditya Prakashan.

Frawley, David. 1993. *Wisdom of the Ancient Seers.* Twin Lakes, Wisconsin: Lotus Press. (Indian edition by Motilal-Banarsidass, New Delhi)

Hancock, Graham. 2002. *Underworld: Flooded Kingdoms of the Ice Age.* London, UK: Penguin Books.

Hicks, H.H. and R.N. Anderson. 1990. Analysis of an Indo-European Vedic-Aryan Head — 4th millennium B.C. *Journal of Indo-European Studies* 18: 425-446.

Jha, N. 1996. *Vedic Glossary on Indus Seals.* Varanasi: Ganga-Kaveri Publishing House.

Jha, N. 1997. 'New Approach to the Study of the Indus Script and Language', edited and translated with notes and comments by N.S. Rajaram. *Quarterly Journal of the Mythic Society* LXXXVI-II. 1 (January-March).

Jha, N. and N.S. Rajaram. 2000. *The Indus Script — A New Direction: Decipherment, Readings, Interpretation.* New Delhi, Voice of India.

Kak, Subhash. 1994. *The Astronomical Code of the Rgveda.* New Delhi: Aditya Prakashan.

Kak, Subhash. 2001. *The Wishing Tree: The Presence and Promise of India.* New Delhi: Munshiram Manoharlal.

Kalyanaraman, Dr. S. 2000. *Sarasvati.* Bangalore: Babasheb Apte Smarak Samiti.

Kisilvid, T. S. Rootsi, M. Metspahi, S. Mastana, K. Kaldma, J. Parik, E. Metspalu, M. Adojan, H.-V. Tolk, V. Stepanov, M. Gölge, E. Usanga, S.S. Papiha, C. Cinni?olu, R. King, L. Cavalli-Sforza, P.A. Unterhill and R. Villems. 'The Genetic Heritage of the Earliest Settlers Persist Both in Indian Tribal and Caste Populations.' 2003. *American Journal of Human Genetics,* 72: pp 313 – 332.

J.B. Kruksal, I. Dyen and P. Black, 'The Vocabulary and Method of Reconstructing Language Trees: Innovations and Large Scale Applications' in *Mathematics in the Archaeological and Historical Sciences* (1971) edited by F.R. Hodson, D.G.

Kendall, and P. Tatu, Edinburgh University Press, Edinburgh.

Lal, B.B. 2005. *The Homeland of the Aryans: Evidence of Rigvedic Flora and Fauna and Archaeology.* New Delhi, Aryan Books International.

Le Mée, Jean, trans. 1975. *Hymns from the Rig-Veda.* New York: Alfred A. Knopf.

Lewontin, Richard. 2000. *Human Diversity* New York: Scientific American Library.

Merton, Robert K., David S. Sills, and Stephen M. Stigler. 1984. The Kelvin dictum and social science: an excursion into the history of an idea. *Journal of the History of the Behavioral Sciences* 20: 319-31.

Misra, S.S. 1992. *The Aryan Problem, a linguistic approach.* New Delhi: Munshiram Manoharlal.

Mukherji, S.N. 1987. *Sir William Jones: a study in eighteenth century British attitudes to India.* Hyderabad: Orient Longmans.

Oppenheimer, Stephen. 2003. *Out of Eden: The Peopling of the World.* London: Constable.

Pargiter, F.E. 1913 (Reissued 1975). *Dynasties of the Kali Age.* Delhi: Deep Publications.

Pargiter, F.E. 1922 (Reissued 1979). *Ancient Indian Traditions.* New Delhi: Cosmo.

Radhakrishna, B.P. and S.S. Mehr, editors (1999) *Vedic Sarasvati: Evolutionary History of a Lost River in Northwest India.* Bangalore: Geological Society of India.

Rajaram, N.S. 1993. *Aryan Invasion of India: The myth and the truth.* New Delhi: Voice of India.

Rajaram, N.S. 1995. *The Politics of History: Aryan invasion theory and the subversion of scholarship.* New Delhi: Voice of India.

Rajaram, N.S. 1996. Jha's Decipherment of the Indus Script. *The Quarterly Journal of the Mythic Society* LXXXVII. 4 (October-December).

Rajaram, N.S. (2002) Sarasvati Ecology and the Vedic Civilization. *The Quarterly Journal of the Mythic Society,* Vol XCIII, Issues 304: July-December 2002.

Rajaram, N.S. 1997. Decipherment of the Indus Script: A Personal Account. *PRAJNA* vol 1, number 3, July-September 1997.

Rajaram, N.S. (2004) *Search for the Historical Krishna.* Bangalore: Prism Books.

Rajaram, N.S. (2004) Population genetics on human migrations. *The Quarterly Journal Of the Mythic Society,* XCV. 3.

Rajaram, N.S. (2005) History as Extension of Natural History, *The Quarterly Journal Of the Mythic Society,* XCVI, 1 – 2.

Rajaram, N.S. and David Frawley. 2001. *Vedic Aryans and the Origins of Civilization,* 3rd edition. New Delhi: Voice of India.

Rao, S.R. 1991. *Dawn and Devolution of the Indus Civilization.* New Delhi: Aditya Prakashan.

Renfrew, Colin. 1990 [1973]. *Before Civilization: The radiocarbon revolution and prehistoric Europe.* London: Penguin [Jonathan Cape].

Rgveda Samhita, Volume I. 1977. Sanskrit text edited and translated by Svami Satya Prakash Sarasvati and Satyakama Vidyalankar, New Delhi: Veda Pratisthana.

Sathe, S. 1991. *Aryans: Who were they?* Mysore: Bharatiya Itihasa Sankalana Samiti.

Sathe, S. 1991a. *Bharateeya Historiography,* 2nd edition. Hyderabad: Bharatiya Itihasa Sankalana Samiti.

Seidenberg, A. 1962. The Ritual Origin of Geometry. *Archive for History of Exact Sciences* 1: 488-527.

Seidenberg, A. 1978. The Origin of Mathematics. *Archive for History of Exact Sciences* 18: 301-42.

Sethna, K.D. 1981. *KARPASA in Prehistoric India: A chronological and cultural clue.* New Delhi: Biblia Impex.

Sethna, K.D. 1992. *The Problem of Aryan Origins: From an Indian point of view.* Second enlarged edition. New Delhi: Aditya Prakashan.

Shaffer, J.G. 1984. Indo-Aryan invasions: cultural myth and archaeological reality. *In* John R. Luckas, ed. *People of South Asia.* New York: Plenum.

Street-Perrott, F.A. and R.A. Perrott. 1990. Abrupt Climate Fluctuations in the Tropics: The Influence of Atlantic Ocean Circulation. *Nature* 343: 607-12.

Talageri, S. 1993. *Aryan Invasion Theory, A reappraisal.* New Delhi: Aditya Prakashan.

Talageri, S. 2000. *The Rigveda: A Historical Analysis.* New Delhi: Aditya Prakashan.

Varma, K.C. 1979. Editorial Note in *Age of the Bharat War,* G.C. Agarawala. New Delhi: Motilal-Banarsidas.

Weiss, H., M-A. Courty, W. Wetterstrom, F. Guichard, L. Senior, R. Meadow and A. Curnow. 1993. Genesis and collapse of third millennium North esopotamian civilization. *Science* 261: 995-1004.

Endnotes

1. Thames and Hudson: London, page 7.

2. *Vedic Aryans and the Origins of Civilization* by Navaratna Rajaram and David Frawley (2001), 3rd edition, New Delhi: Voice of India; pages 176-7.

3. Much of the ancient Mahabharat devotes itself to the *Raja Dharma* or the way of kings, which forms an entire section of the Shanti Parva.

4. Like the Aryan Invasion theory that has India borrow its ancient Vedic literature from a non-Indian source from Central Asia or Europe.

5. The Aitareya Upanishad and Aranyaka show this quite well.

6. Questionable racial and linguistic theories, like the Aryan Invasion, either not based upon or even contrary to archaeological and other scientific evidence, have dominated the discourse. Or Marxist theories based upon modern ideas of politics and economics have been imposed on ancient peoples, ignoring the natural setting in which they lived. We will examine these in more detail later.

7. Western theories like the Aryan Invasion theory that has the main culture or peoples of ancient India come from the northwest are contrary to the facts of the geography and natural history of the region that is connected more to Southeast Asia.

8. Most Western views of the history of India fail to take into account the natural history or the geographical ties of India, which have always been to the south and the east.

9. This is another reason why the idea that India needed outside populations to provide its people or its culture makes little sense.

10. The *Jambudvipa* of the Purans.

11. Chapter 40 of the *Vajasaneyi Samhita,* which later became an independent text as the famous *Isha Upanishad.*

12. Geneticists like L. Cavalli-Sforza and S. Oppenheimer have noted that settlers in the coastal regions of India were the source ('inocula') for the population of India. Some of them later migrated northwards and westward to populate Europe. This is the exact reverse of the various migration-invasion theories (like the Aryan invasion) advanced by linguists and anthropologists who sought to derive Indians and their civilization from Central Asia, Eurasia or even Europe. See for example, *Eden in the East* by Stephen Oppenheimer (2003), London: Constable. This is discussed in more detail in later chapters.

13. This does not mean that there were no non-African humans before the Toba Explosion, but only that descendants of those earlier populations have not survived outside of Africa. Apparently another group out of Africa 120,000 years ago made its way to Egypt but disappeared 90,000 years ago without leaving a genetic trace.

14. See *Out of Eden: The peopling of the world* by Stephen Oppenheimer (2003). Constable, London.

15. The Genetic Heritage of the Earliest Settlers Persist Both in Indian Tribal and Caste Populations: by T. Kisilvid, S. Rootsi, M. Metspahi, S. Mastana, K. Kaldma, J. Parik, E. Metspalu, M. Adojan, H.-V. Tolk, V. Stepanov, M. Gölge, E. Usanga, S.S. Papiha, C. Cinni?olu, R. King, L. Cavalli-Sforza, P.A. Unterhill and R. Villems. 2003. *American Journal of Human Genetics,* 72: pp 313 – 332.

16. It is found among other people also, including in pre-Columbian Native American tribes. The Nazis probably got their swastika symbol from ancient Roman ruins like Pompey where also it is found rather than directly from India.

17. See: Genetic Evidence on the Origin of Indian Caste Populations by M. Bamshad, T. Kivisild, W.S. Watkins, M.E. Dixon, C.E. Ricker, B.B. Rao, J.M. Naidu, B.V.R. Prasad, P.G. Reddy, A. Rasanagam, et al. 2001, *Genome Research* 11, pp 994 – 1004.

The Cavalli-Sforza et al. article above was meant partly as a rebuttal of the Bamshad et al. article.

18. See for example, Enard et al., 'Molecular evolution of FOXP2, a gene involved in speech and language', *Nature* 418, 869 – 872, (2002). While a good deal remains to be learnt, particularly with regard to the time scales involved, it definitely rules out the 5000 years or so postulated by linguists and anthropologists. This means theories claiming a recent non-Indian origin for the people and languages of India. (See notes 1, 2 and 7 above.)

19. The Vocabulary and Method of Reconstructing Language Trees: Innovations and Large Scale Applications by J.B. Kruksal, I. Dyen and P. Black, in *Mathematics in the Archaeological and Historical Sciences* (1971) edited by F.R. Hodson, D.G. Kendall, and P. Tatu, Edinburgh University Press, Edinburgh.

20. *Great Human Diasporas,* Addison-Wesley, 1995: page 190.

21. Curiously Asko Parpola regards the Vedic people as an earlier offshoot of the Scythians whom Bishop Caldwell makes into the Dravidians!

22. Attempts were made at first, especially in the 19th century, to derive all achievements from the Greeks but discoveries in Egypt and Mesopotamia made this impossible. Efforts continue in Western academia to prove that Indian and other non-European achievements in mathematics and astronomy were borrowings from the Greeks. We will examine this issue later in the book and show its inaccuracy. The Greeks were a late ancient people who were better at saving and preserving, rather than inventing the knowledge of the ancient world.

23. Most recorded population movements in ancient times have been in search of warmer and wetter climates or to avoid floods and catastrophes. The mass migration out of Africa 80,000 years ago was due to the onset of the Ice Age when large parts of Africa turned arid making it unsuitable for human habitation.

24. This is not a bolt from the blue. Other writers have noted the impact of natural history and early importance of maritime activity. These include: *The Long Summer* by Brian Fagan and *Eden in the East* by Stephen Oppenheimer. In his book *Gods, Sages and Kings,* David Frawley had noted the mar-

itime symbolizm in the Vedas as far back as 1991, while Rajaram has highlighted the importance of natural history and climate changes, and their record in Indian literature in several articles. See: Rajaram, N.S. (2205) History as Extension of Natural History, *The Quarterly Journal Of the Mythic Society,* XCVI, 1 – 2.

25. *The Long Summer* by Brian Fagan, *op. cit.*, pages 93 – 4.

26. In their work *Rice: Then and Now,* R.E. Huke and E.H. Huke observe that the latest evidence shows that agriculture began with rice cultivation in Southeast Asia before 10,000 BCE and not with wheat and barley in the Fertile Crescent. International Rice Research Institute, 1990.

27. Geneticists like S. Oppenheimer have noted that there is high frequency of East Asian genetic markers in both South and North India. See *Eden in the East* by Stephen Oppenheimer (1999), Phoenix, London. Page 265. The book errs by accepting the Aryan invasion theory as proven. This is corrected in his later book *Out of Eden.*

28. Note also Jaiminiya Brahmana III.99 for further allusions to the flood.

29. This is a straightforward account of Manu and the flood of which there are other variations. The flood is a scientific fact, with sea levels higher today by 400 feet. It is receiving archaeological support also. Marine archaeologists have found man-made underwater structures in the Gulf of Khambat off the Gujarat coast as well as near Poompahar and Mahabalipuram off the Tamil Nadu coast. Some of these have been dated to 7500 BCE or nearly 10,000 years old. The full extent of the flood damage in India and Southeast Asia will never be known.

30. RV VI.61; VII.95; VII.96

31. In referring to passages in the Rig Veda, the first term (in Roman letters) indicates the book or the *mandala,* the second the hymn or the *sukta,* and the third the verse of the mantra. For example, X.75.5 refers to mantra 5 in *sukta* 75 from the tenth book or *mandala* X of the Rig Veda.

32. RV VII.36.6, *sarasvatā saptathā sindhumàtà*

33. RV VI.52.6, *sarasvatā sindhubhià pinvamànà*

34. RV VI.61.14, *mà tvat kìetràçyaraçàni ganma*

35. A few scholars today argue that there was no Sarasvati river at all in the historical period. The problem for that view is that there are numerous ruins along the dried banks of the river. These would not be there if there was no water in the river! Such a view is nonsensical.

36. The Harappan civilization ended around 1900 BC, not 1500 BC as stated in some history books.

37. RV I.32.12; I.34.8; I.35.8; I.71.7; I.102.2; I.141.2; I.164.3; I.191.14; II.12.3; III.1.4; IV.28.1; V.43.1; VI.61.10; VII.7.6; VII.18.24; VII.67.8; VIII.24.27; VIII.41.2, 9; VIII.54.4; VIII.69.12; VIII.96.1; IX.54.2; IX.66.6; IX.86.21, 36; IX.92.4; X.13.5; X.43.3; X.49.9; X.64.8; X.67.12; X.104.8

38. Main Rivers mentioned in the Rig Veda: Book I—Sindhu (126.1), Sarasvati (3.10-12; 164.49), Jahnavi (Ganga; 116.18-19), Rasa (112.12); Book II—Sarasvati (41.16-18); Book III—Vipas

(33), Shutudri (33), Sarasvati (23.4), Drishadvati (23.4), Apaya (23.4) Jahnavi (Ganga; 59.6); Book IV— Sindhu (43.6), Asikni (17.15), Vipas (30.11), Parushni (22.2) Saryu (30.18), Rasa (43.6); Book V—Rasa (41.15; 53.9), Anitabha (53.9), Kubha (53.9), Krumu (V.53.9), Gomati (61.19), Sindhu (53.9), Parushni (52.9), Sarasvati (43.11), Yamuna (52.17), Saryu (53.9); Book VI—Sarasvati (52.6; 61.1-14), Ganga (45.31); Book VII— Asikni (5.3), Parushni (18.8), Sarasvati (36.6, 95.1-6; 96.1-6), Yamuna (18.19); Book VIII—Gomati (24.30), Suvastu (19.37), Sindhu (20.24-25; 25.12, 26.18), Sushoma (53.11), Asikni (20.24), Parushni (74.15), Sarasvati (21.17-18; 54.4), Amsumati (Yamuna, 96.14-15); Book IX—Rasa (41.6), Sarasvati (67.32) ; Book X—Trishtama (75.6), Susartu (75.6), Rasa (75.6: 108; 121.4), Shveta (75.6), Sindhu (64.9; 75.6), Kubha (75.6), Krumu (75.6), Gomati (75.6), Mehatnu (75.6), Arjikiya (75.5), Sushoma (75.5), Vitasta (75.5), Marudvridha (75.5), Asikni (75.5), Parushni (75.5), Shutudri (75.5), Sarasvati (30.12; 64.9; 75.5), Yamuna (75.5), Ganga (75.5), Saryu (64.9)

39. RV VI.45.31; V.53.9; X.61.9

40. Refer to Frawley's *Gods, Sages and Kings*, and *Rig Veda and the History of India* for a complete listing of these oceanic references to the Vedic deities.

41. RV I.164.42; IX.33.6; X.47.20

42. RV I.161.14: VI.50.13; VI.72.3; VII.70.2; VIII.20.25; IX.80.1

43. *à antàd à paràrdhàt pêthivyai samudraparyantàyà ekaràäiti*

44. Another branch of the Yadus lived in Mathura; the Yamuna served as a river link between the Kurus and the Yadus of the Mathura branch. These were the Bharat Yadus.

45. This greater extent of Harappan India is another reason why we cannot simply turn India into a satellite of cultures to the west.

46. Refer to the *Homeland of the Aryans: Evidence of Rig Vedic Flora and Fauna and* Archaeology by B.B. Lal for an detailed discussion of this topic.

47. This is described in *The Deciphered Indus Script* (2000) by N. Jha and N.S. Rajaram, New Delhi: Aditya Prakashan. Had scholars been willing to drop the "Harappans as non-Vedic" dogma, the script might have been understood 50 years earlier. Jha not only ignored the dogma, he had the scholarship and perseverance to make the breakthrough.

48. A single example of pre-Harappan writing is known. Rajaram's decipherment proposes it to be a reference to the Rig Veda. The artifact carrying the inscription has been dated to 3500 BCE, or as early as writing in Sumeria. This also agrees with our dating – of Rig Veda as pre-Harappan. See 'Harappan and pre-Harappan writing,' by N.S. Rajaram and N. Jha in *The Quarterly Journal of the Mythic Society*. Vol. XC, No. 3: 59 – 78 (July – September 1999).

49. We are greatly indebted to Dr. Natwar Jha for his deep insights into the Vedic symbolizm contained in Harappan iconography as well as in numerous messages resulting from his decipherment.

50. According to Jha's decipherment, it may be read as *panca-svasti adma*, or *panca-svasti vidma*. The former means nourished by *panca svasti,* and the latter means knower of *panca svasti*

51. Refer to Jha and Rajaram, *the Deciphered Indus Script* page 74.

52. Rajaram and Jha's proposed reading on the seal is *ishadyatah marah*. Mara is the force that causes the destruction of the universe. The message of the seal is: Ishvara controls Mara. The seated yogi (in *mula-bandhasana*) is Ishvara. Ishvara is Pashupati.

53. Yoga is much older than the celebrated *Yoga Sutra* by Patanjali, which is a compilation at a later era. It is likely that some Sutra works are of the Harappa Era. Even Patanjali's Sutras may not have been the first on Yoga.

54. There are some stray varieties that differ somewhat but are not relevant here.

55, RV I.162.18, *catustriœiad vàjino devabandhor vaèkràr aívasya*

56. RV I.163.1, *yad akrandaâ prathamam jàyamàna udyant samudràt uta và puràiàt*

57. See the *Homeland of the Aryans: Evidence of* Rig Vedic *Flora and Fauna and* Archaeology by B.B. Lal pp. 80-81.

58. It is worth noting that very ancient fossils of 17-ribbed equs knows as *Equs sivalensis* have been found in the Himalayan foothills or the Siwaliks. These could be ancestors of the Indian breed.

59. The dates may differ slightly depending on the methodology and the sources used. See *Climate Change: A Multidisciplinary Approach* by William James Burroughs (2001), Cambridge University Press. Cambridge, England. A slightly different version is given in *The Long Summer: How Climate Changed Civilization* by Brian Fagan (2004). Basic Books: New York. The differences, which are minor, could be due to the method used for correcting radiocarbon dates. For early dates, Fagan uses coral growth rings instead of the more conventional tree ring data.

60. Yet note that even if the date of Krishna came later in the historical period, it would not change the Vedic nature of ancient India or the general flow of history. The key is when the Yamuna began to flow through Mathura, the city of Krishna. Krishna must be placed after this date. So far it is not clear when that was, either in the fourth or third millennium BCE.

61. See the work of Subhash Kak for more information on the mathematical symbolizm of the numbering of these Vedic books, particularly his *Astronomical Code of the Rigveda*.

62. Seidenberg, A. 1978. The Origin of Mathematics. *Archive for History of Exact Sciences* 18: 301-42.

63. See Subhash Kak's article, The Speed of Light and Puranic Cosmology.

Index

ABOUT THE AUTHORS

Dr. David Frawley (Vamadava Shastri), is one of the few Westerners recognized in India as a Vedacharya or teacher of the ancient Vedic wisdom. His field of study includes Ayurveda, Yoga and Vedant and the greater Hindu and Vedic tradition. He is regarded as an important commentator on Hinduism (Sanatan Dharma) and its contemporary challenges. He has also done an extensive examination of the Vedas, including a revision of ancient history in the light of new archaeological finds and a more spiritual approach to Vedic texts. Dr. Frawley has written more than twenty books and numerous articles over the last twenty years, published both in India and the West. He also lectures throughout India on a yearly basis. Presently, he is director of the American Institute of Vedic Studies, PO Box 8357, Santa Fe, New Mexico, 87504-8357, USA.

Dr. Navaratna S. Rajaram is a mathematician, linguist and historian who after a twenty-year career as an academic and industrial researcher in the United States turned his attention to history, in which he has several notable achievements. He is the author of the acclaimed book *Vedic Aryans and the Origins of Civilization* (with David Frawley). He collaborated with renowned Vedic scholar Dr. Natwar Jha on the decipherment of the 5,000-year-old Indus script leading to their joint work *The Deciphered Indus Script*. In May 1999, Rajaram deciphered the newly discovered sample of what has been called the 'world's oldest writing', showing it to be related to the Rig Veda. In recent years, he has pioneered the use of natural history and genetics in the study of ancient history. He has also written extensively on Indian history, philosophy and current affairs. He is one of the world's most widely read authors on these subjects.

ABOUT THE PUBLISHERS

Swaminarayan Aksharpith is the publishing house of the Bochasanwasi Shri Akshar Purushottam Swaminarayan Sanstha (BAPS), which is a global socio-spiritual NGO with over 9,000 centres committed to the social, moral and spiritual uplift of mankind.

The BAPS is a charitable NGO in Consultative Status with the Economic and Social Council of the United Nations. Its world renowned cultural and spiritual complexes like Swaminarayan Akshardham in Gandhinagar and New Delhi and the Swaminarayan Mandirs in London, Houston and Chicago, are some of its epoch-making contributions to society.

Under the inspiration and guidance of Pramukh Swami Maharaj, BAPS has earned an endearing and unique place in the hearts of millions throughout the world. Acclaimed as a unique and rare holy soul of India, Pramukh Swami Maharaj is the fifth successor in the illustrious spiritual tradition of Bhagwan Swaminarayan and the embodiment of the universal Hindu ideals.

In his presence doubts dissolve, confusions clear, hurts heal and the mind finds peace. His selfless love and morality equally soothes and inspires morality in children, youths and the aged; regardless of caste, creed or status.

His striking humility, simplicity and spirituality have touched many religious and national leaders. Above all, his profound experience and realization of God is the essence of his success and divine lustre.